Beyond Strength

Beyond Strength

Psychological Profiles of
Olympic Athletes

Steven Ungerleider, Ph.D.

Jacqueline M. Golding, Ph.D.

 Wm. C. Brown Publishers

Cover design and interior design by Gordon Stromberg
Copyedited by Mary M. Palmborg
Artwork and cover photo by John Subert

Library of Congress Catalog Card Number: 90–86354

ISBN 0–697–12058–9

Printed in the United States of America by Wm. C. Brown Publishers,
2460 Kerper Boulevard, Dubuque, IA 52001

10 9 8 7 6 5 4 3 2 1

*to my parents and to my children.
As I have inherited genes of
athleticism, I now pass to my
children the environmental concerns
of good sportsmanship.*

su

*to Jim,
my life partner and workout buddy
who knows about balance.*

jmg

Bio Sketch

Steven Ungerleider completed his undergraduate work at the University of Texas, Austin, where he also competed as a collegiate gymnast. He holds a Ph.D. from the University of Oregon and is a licensed psychologist and Director of Integrated Research Services, Incorporated in Eugene. In addition to his clinical responsibilities, Ungerleider has been the recipient of several Alcohol Drug Abuse Mental Health Administration (ADAMHA) and U.S. Department of Education grant awards and has published many journal articles on substance abuse prevention. In 1984, he was appointed to the United States Olympic Committee Sport Psychology Registry which assists elite athletes with performance issues. Ungerleider is a consultant to several sports organizations and recently completed an alcohol and other drug prevention evaluation for the NBA Los Angeles Lakers. When not in his office, he may be found jogging and running whitewater rivers with his wife, playing tennis with his oldest daughter, or at the National Academy of Artistic Gymnastics, observing his youngest child.

Jacqueline M. Golding is a social psychologist and faculty member at the University of California, San Francisco. She holds a Ph.D. from the University of California, Los Angeles, and earned her bachelor's degree at Yale. Golding has published widely in the scientific literature on topics such as the epidemiology of psychological problems, especially depression and alcohol-related problems; the relation of stress and social resources to individual distress; psychological aspects of physical health; and the psychology of women. She has also published several articles on sport psychology in professional journals, focusing on mental practice, dreaming, mood states, and social support. She is a recreational bicyclist and has participated in century rides, running events, and triathlons.

Contents

Foreword

When I first met Dr. Steven Ungerleider in Eugene, Oregon, prior to the 1984 Olympics, I was very pleased to learn that he and other psychologists were exploring the benefits and usefulness of visualization. I have always felt that visualization and creating a positive mental attitude can make a good athlete a great one. I discussed with Steven my experiences in competition as a result of my visualization techniques which led to my victory in the high jump at the 1968 Mexico City Olympic Games.

I began to develop my new style using the "Fosbury Flop" in 1963, at Medford Senior High School in Medford, Oregon. The style developed during competition when my body seemed to react to the challenge of the bar. I became charged by the desire and will to achieve success. Slowly I experimented with this new physical sensation which ultimately led to a new technique in the high jump.

At Oregon State University, I continued to work on this new method of jumping as well as my images and visualization strategies associated with this new technique. As the style was developed in competition, I began to develop a thought process in order to repeat a successful jump.

Several years into college, I developed a process in preparing for a jump in which I would: (1) "psych" myself up; (2) create a picture; (3) "feel" a successful jump—the perfect jump; and (4) develop a positive attitude to make the jump. Once I had developed the Flop style and my coaches taught me strength training, my Olympic Gold Medal success would come from the visualization and imaging process.

Every good athlete has his or her own individual physical assets, attributes, and desires. I strongly believe that we can best achieve our human potential with the use of positive visualization and mental imaging. It is my hope that this book by Steven Ungerleider and

Jacqueline Golding will help to communicate these techniques to the psychologists, trainers, coaches, athletes, and others who may assist young athletes with fulfilling their potential as well-rounded competitors.

Dick Fosbury
July, 1990

Preface

This book is written and intended for professionals who deal with athletes at all skill levels. The data examined here were derived from a study of elite athletes and may be useful for coaches, trainers, athletes, psychologists, and sports medicine professionals. *BEYOND STRENGTH: PSYCHOLOGICAL PROFILES OF OLYMPIC ATHLETES* is written for the professional sport psychology consultant as well as the individual athlete who wants to enhance his or her performance. This book may be used as a springboard for professionals who want to understand more about the profile of the elite track and field athlete. This book offers very practical explanations derived from a comprehensive research project on elite competitors. The data found here are derived from the largest applied research project ever conducted among United States Olympic track and field athletes. Our sample included all qualifiers in forty-three track and field events who were invited to their respective trials for the 1988 Olympics in Seoul, South Korea. The data have been analyzed over the past several years (since the Olympic Games) and are now presented in practical, nonacademic language. Theoretical concepts are introduced, supported by a comprehensive bibliography, and practical explanations are given, including personal insights into the how's and why's of elite competitors.

The purpose of this book is to provide new insight into the psychological training strategies of elite athletes. It is written in a nontechnical style, but offers empirical information regarding the motivation, dedication, moods, and training styles of elite track and field athletes. The book is based on our findings from the 1988 study which was conducted under the auspices of The Athletics Congress with guidance from the United States Olympic Committee.

The rationale behind the organization of the book is based on a logical set of constructs within the sport psychology field. Our research evaluated several areas of concern involving the "total" athlete and his/her preparation for personal best performances. We asked how, when, and why athletes used mental practice, visualization, special training routines, and/or stress management strategies. We also looked at how athletes maintained a level of normal functioning during a relatively stressful period in their lives. To whom did they turn for emotional support? What were their reasons for striving so hard to attain their athletic goals? All of these questions are discussed in an organized fashion based on our findings from the survey research as well as in-depth interviews with a sample of Olympians.

Our theme is clearly the ELITE ATHLETE and how he/she utilizes psychological strategies for performance enhancement. Our approach to the subject is unique because of the quality and breadth of data from our Elite Athlete Project. We hope that this book will provide a data base that will enhance the existing literature within the sport psychology field. We have attempted to be clear and cogent in our descriptors of methods and techniques used by elite athletes. When possible, we offer specific examples of a practical application in training. Where appropriate, we cite examples of individuals who used a mental practice strategy, visualization, or meditation to alter their negative mind-set in preparation for the race of their life. Although we focus on psychological characteristics and strategies of elite athletes, we hope that athletes at all levels of competition, and the professionals who work with them, will find useful information here.

Our text is divided into seven chapters, each addressing unique but interrelated components within the sport psychology field. These topical areas include the characteristics of elite competitors; mental preparation strategies; dreaming and daydreaming; mood profiles and states; stress, injury, and illness; coping and social support; and substance abuse prevention and performance enhancement in a drug-free environment. Each chapter will begin with a literature review, followed by data from the Elite Athlete Project, discussion of appropriate instruments or diagnostic strategies, and, finally, a chapter summary and references.

Acknowledgments

Our thanks to the hundreds of Olympic trials participants who shared their experiences and their insights into the psychology of athletic competition by completing surveys or responding to telephone interviews we conducted as part of the Elite Athlete Project. Without their participation, this book would not have been possible.

We also want to express our appreciation to our colleagues, especially those special people at Integrated Research Services, Inc. They include Tracy Johnson, Mary Ellen Gonzalez, Colette Kimball, Martin Molof, Ph.D., Jack Dresser, Ph.D., Sara Gutierres, Ph.D., Robert J. Hogg, M.B.A., and Integrated Research advisors Richard Borgman, William Mason, C.P.A., Richard Hart, Michael Levin, and Tom Barkin. A very special thanks to our systems analyst and statistician, Stefan Kramer, for his tremendous diligence and patience with both authors. Acknowledgments go to John Subert and J. P. Dusseault of Industrial Litho, Inc. for their creative graphics. Patrick Jennings, our fabulous research assistant, deserves many thanks for his tremendous contribution to our book.

We would like to express our gratitude to Berny Wagner, former National Coordinator for The Athletics Congress, Duffy Mahoney of TAC and his wonderful support staff, including Barbara James, in Indianapolis. Their interest and cooperation on the Elite Athlete Project insured its success from the outset. Many thanks to Kelly Jensen, a former Olympic trials finalist and National team member in the steeplechase, for his insight, liaison, and friendship on this project.

We also thank Robert Voy, M.D., Jerry May, Ph.D., the late Dorothy Harris, Ph.D., Bruce Ogilvie, Ph.D., and Diane O'Rourke, Ph.D. for their initial review and insightful comments on earlier drafts of our manuscript. Sincere appreciation is extended to Ed Bartell, our senior editor at Wm. C. Brown Publishers, for his guidance throughout the project.

As athletes turn to consult their coaches, psychologists often look to their teachers, guides, and mentors. In this regard, we express our respect and gratitude to several important people. Appreciation is extended to Professors Martin Acker and Henry Dizney, J. Thomas Ungerleider, M.D., Professor Milton Rosenbaum, M.D., Audrey Burnam, Ph.D., and Professors Marvin Karno, Jerome L. Singer, Faye Crosby, and Leigh Burstein. Special thanks to Lisa Marmor, Ph.D. and Jon Marmor for their friendship and athletic inspiration.

Finally, Dr. Ungerleider thanks his wife, Sharon, and two talented daughters, Shoshana and Ariel, for their love, insight, and support during obsessive-compulsive research/writing binges! Dr. Golding thanks her husband, Jim, and her cats, Zonker and Pepper, for their love, support, patience, and humor during the writing of this book.

Beyond Strength

CHAPTER 1

"It's interesting when you speak of role models for sport. My dad is 68 years old and is still pole vaulting. My son, who is just two, runs around with a little pole that a pole company made for him. My dad who jumps 9'9" still has a place in his backyard, and that's the way it was growing up; there was always a place to practice. I have three older brothers and you might say that my dad's influence and just the luck of having three older siblings who were vaulters, played a big part in creating an image of the sport. So before I even started jumping at an early age, I had already been watching them for many years. And I learned early on, at the ripe old age of five, quality techniques for enhancement . . . that is what you were supposed to do, and what you weren't supposed to do."

Earl Bell
Four Time Olympian
Pole Vault

The Psychology of Sport Entering the 1990s

The past decade has seen dramatic systemic changes in the way athletes compete at the elite levels. Coaches, trainers, sport consultants, and medical personnel have all played an important role in the evolution of sport with changes occurring both at the individual athlete level and within the institution of the respective governing bodies (Ogilvie & Tutko, 1971; Ogilvie, 1974, 1979). Individual athletes are using more alternative strategies including mental practice and visualization; and institutions are supporting specialized training sessions at various training centers to enhance the experience of the "whole" athlete. As our culture demands more winning and success of our young athletes, new, innovative, and creative training strategies are sought. Coaches constantly search for new levels of performance and simultaneously try to avoid overtraining, injury, and burnout.

Eastern bloc countries have been using a series of well-documented mental practice/cognitive strategies as a regular part of their training routine for some twenty-five years. According to Dr. Gerd Konzag, a noted East German sports scientist interviewed in *The Sport Psychologist* (Roberts & Kimiecik, 1989), these strategies are not only taught to athletes, but are first implemented with coaching staff. This style of teaching/training differs dramatically from our Western model. In the United States, we work with athletes first (and sometimes exclusively) and hope that coaches will facilitate the process of implementing new training strategies in daily workout schedules. Although U.S. coaches and trainers are becoming more receptive to sport psychology interventions, there is still widespread suspicion and lack of confidence about the use of mental practice strategies among their ranks and consultation of sport psychologists is stigmatized (Linder, Pillow & Reno, 1988). According to a recent report compiled by the United States Olympic Committee Sports Psychology Division, coaches are not always willing to allow outside professionals to enter the training milieu (Murphy & Ferrante, 1989). We hope that this book will provide a foundation for new strategies and assist coaches in reducing their resistance to performance enhancement strategies.

Ironically, we found many athletes in our study who trained without coaches and yet had designed very innovative mental practice strategies into their daily training. It is not clear whether these strategies were derived from earlier coaching experiences (high school or college, etc.) or absorbed from the popular press. The media, as well as the research literature, seem to be providing no shortage of alternative strategies for elite athletic training. Shortly after the Olympic Games in Seoul, South Korea, an article appeared on the New York Times Op/Ed page headlined, "At the Olympics, Soviet Mind Games." It was written by Grigori Raiport (1988), president of the Russian Success Method and a psychologist who was trained at the Moscow National Research Institute of Physical Culture.

Dr. Raiport noted that:

> "Russian athletes learned long ago that while the human body has its natural limits, the mind's potential is unlimited. The strategic goal of Soviet sport psychology, however, is to elicit peak performance from athletes. To that end Russians analyzed the nature of athletic inspiration and discovered that it consists of three components: physical, emotional (moods and feelings), and mental thoughts. When inspired, most athletes would experience diverse physical sensations such as a tingling jaw, coolness in the temples, and lightness of the body. The Russian method is to train athletes to reproduce those symptoms at will, using autoconditioning. This technique helps an athlete choose his optimal mood for a competition, be it joy, happiness, or anger. Even such a negative emotion as sorrow can be used constructively."

Dr. Raiport noted that any strong emotion possesses energy, and therefore coaches might even transform the negative energy of grief into a constructive force. His reference in the newspaper article was to the outstanding American speed skater, Dan Jansen, who lost his sister to an untimely death during his finals at the 1988 Winter Games in Calgary.

Transforming negative images to positive ones, replacing old visual cues with new, performance-enhanced ones, and using one's dreams to map interventions for winning events, seem to be the agenda for the psychology of sport entering the 1990s. However, most of us are keenly aware of another agenda which lies on the other end of the performance spectrum. Substance abuse, including use of chemicals intended to enhance performance, seems to be quite pervasive in sport. This chemical strategy, used by athletes from the ranks of junior high school teams to the elite competitor and professional athlete, seems to create a counterforce to competition within the legal, moral, and ethical guidelines of United States and international governing bodies.

For the past decade, including the Seoul games of Autumn 1988, many professionals who work in sports-related fields have been besieged with reports of substance abuse, illegal performance-enhancing techniques, and rumors of steroids. It seems that for every single great athletic performance, we read about ten performances that are drug-assisted. A recent editorial in a national newspaper suggested that in 1992 (Barcelona Olympics), we hold two Olympic Games: one drug induced and one chemical free! Since 1988, many dramatic changes have occurred in random drug testing, verification procedures, and International Olympic Committee rulings. In our final chapter, we review some of these changes. Although the emphasis of this book is strategies that focus on cognitive, emotional, and behavioral interventions for performance enhancement, a major theme throughout the text is sport in a drug-free and healthful, competitive environment.

THE DESIGN OF THE STUDY

The Elite Athlete Project involved 1,200 Olympic hopefuls who qualified to participate in the United States Olympic track and field trials in April 1988. These elite athletes were preparing for the 1988 Seoul Olympic Games, and after years of preparation were now approaching a critical competition, the U.S. trials. All athletes in our study had qualified according to TAC (The Athletics Congress) standards and were formally invited to their respective events. The Olympic trials for the women's marathon took place on May 1, 1988, in Pittsburgh, Pennsylvania, and the men's trials took place on April 24, 1988, in Jersey City, New Jersey. All other events (a total of forty-three for combined track, field, and marathon) took place in Indianapolis, Indiana, in July 1988. Athletes were surveyed in April 1988, before all trials, and again after the Olympic Games, in November 1988.

With the approval of The Athletics Congress, the national governing body for track and field, Integrated Research Services, Inc., undertook sixteen months of preparation for a mail survey of all eligible elite track and field qualifiers. A sixteen-page, 240-item instrument was designed in collaboration with The Athletics Congress staff and submitted to a human subjects review committee. The survey instrument included items concerning demographic characteristics, physical and mental training strategies including the use of imagery and visualization, injury experience, mood profiles, motivations for competition, social support, and stress measures. The instrument used in November was almost identical to the first one (sent in April 1988) with the exception that athletes were asked about training strategies and other experiences and behaviors "since July 1988." In June 1990, phone interviews were conducted with the informed consent of both TAC and sixteen Olympic athletes. These structured interviews were conducted by the first author, Steven Ungerleider, as a follow-up to the survey research data collected earlier.

To protect the confidentiality of the athletes, no names were permitted on the survey instruments and no individual athlete name or address was released to the research team. All instruments were prepared by Integrated Research and then mailed to TAC headquarters in Indiana for appropriate labeling with the athlete names and addresses. A number code was attached to the instrument so that the researchers could match responses from both waves of data collection (pre-Olympic trials and post-Olympic Games). Athletes were informed that participation in the study was strictly voluntary. A cover letter from TAC supporting the research endeavor, and a stamped return envelope were included in the mailing. After five weeks, a reminder letter was sent to all athletes asking them to complete the instrument if they had not already done so. Four weeks after the first reminder, a postcard was sent to all athletes thanking them for their cooperation in the study.

Of the 1,200 survey instruments mailed, 633 were returned constituting a valid response rate of 53% for the pre-Olympic survey, and 450 were returned for a response rate of 38% for

7

the post-Olympic study. Many of our data analyses were based on the 633 responses to the pre-Olympic survey. When we examined changes between pre- (April) and post- (November) surveys, only the 373 athletes who answered both surveys were included in the analyses.

CHARACTERISTICS OF THE SAMPLE

Women (52%) and men (48%) were about equally represented in the sample. The majority of the sample were single (59%), nearly a third married (31%), and a small group (3%) divorced. Nearly a quarter of the respondents had some college education, nearly one-half were college graduates, and 28% held graduate school degrees. The average athlete had begun competing in his/her event by 1980, some eight years before the Olympic trials. About half of the athletes competed in their event in high school, two-thirds competed in college, and nearly as many post college. Thirty-two athletes reported competing in their event before high school and 76% of the respondents competed in sports other than track and field. Nearly a third competed in other sports at the college level, five athletes competed in other sports at the Olympic level, and four were professional athletes in other sports at some time in their career.

Average training per week for elite competitors was seventeen hours. For track and running athletes, the average training miles per month was 238. The average continuous training run was sixteen miles with some athletes logging as much as thirty-four miles in a workout. Three-quarters of the athletes kept a log of their training and competition. Nearly all athletes did interval training, four-fifths trained on streets, two-thirds trained on trails, most used the track, and one-half used all three modes. The busiest time of day for track athletes was between 3:00 and 6:00 P.M. when half did their training. Only two athletes ran after 9:00 P.M. The majority of athletes worked out alone and about two-thirds did weight training in addition to their running work. Seventy-two elite athletes reported fear or anxiety about training alone. Almost 70% of the respondents have had a coach for an average period of 6.3 years. Two-thirds of the sample reported that their parents had between "none and moderate" influence on their decision to compete. Thirty athletes noted that their parents had "extreme" influences. Fathers had the most significant influence on the career path of these elite athletes.

One-quarter of the respondents reported that the greatest sacrifice they made in the previous two years in order to train for the Olympic trials was in their personal relationships. One-fifth noted financial sacrifice, with almost as many reporting career-related sacrifices. Three-quarters reported that the above mentioned sacrifice had caused "moderate to extreme stress" in their lives. Athletes were most likely to anticipate that *not* making the Olympic team would adversely affect their emotional well-being (expected by one-half of the athletes), followed by one-seventh who felt their self-worth would be hurt, and nearly one-seventh who said they would experience financial impact. In *making* the Olympic team, two-fifths of the sample said the greatest benefit would be emotional; one-third said the greatest benefit would be increased self-worth, and one-seventh reported better career opportunities. Fewer than one-tenth ranked financial gain as the most important benefit of becoming an Olympian. Eighty-five percent of the respondents said they had a "moderate" to "intense" commitment to making the team. Surprisingly, ninety-four athletes said that they either had "no" or "very little" commitment to becoming an Olympian.

DEMOGRAPHIC AND ATHLETIC CHARACTERISTICS OF TRACK, FIELD, AND MARATHON ATHLETES

Of the 633 athletes in forty-three total events, 267 specialized in track events (other than marathon), 197 in the marathon, and 128 in field events, with some athletes participating in more than one event. In most events there was an even distribution of male and female athletes with the exception of the marathon. More than twice as many women participated in the marathon trials. All field events, and track events up to the 400 meters, were reported as the most prevalent activities during high school years. Only forty-one athletes ran the marathon in high school. At the college level, participation in both track and field events shifted significantly. Nearly 90% of our respondents reported some track activity (over 400 meters) during college athletics. After college, marathon participation was significantly increased, including 70% of our sample who ran at least one marathon. Two athletes actually reported running a marathon before high school. The largest body of athletes in any event who competed outside the track and field arena, including NBA basketball, were high jumpers and pole vaulters.

Athletes competing in different events, or those with different demographic attributes, sometimes had different patterns of athletic characteristics. For example, field competitors were more likely to keep logs of their training and competition than track athletes. Those who had prior high school and college competition experience were more likely to use mental practice strategies. Age was also a significant predictor of certain types of athletic training. Because marathoners are typically older athletes, age became a significant factor in many of our analyses.

At least two perspectives are possible in interpreting differences between athletes who did and did not qualify for the Olympic team. From one perspective, many of the differences between these two groups may be very fine and subtle. All athletes who were invited to the Olympic trials underwent rigorous training in order to meet the qualifying standard of the United States trials. In many ways, qualifying and nonqualifying athletes were more alike than different and as a result, small and subtle differences might account for team selection on the day of the track and field trials. It seems reasonable to infer that the trials are intended as a measure of "ultimate" performance, although most people, including elite level coaches, feel that one round of performance is a less than perfect measure. However, there may have been random, unpredictable factors operating the day of the trials that affected team selection. These differences may, in fact, be so small that on any given day team selection could fluctuate several times. On the other hand, selection to the United States Olympic Track and Field Team itself may, in some sense, be more important than exact "ultimate" performance level. Many athletes and coaches are concerned with winning the event (whether it be a qualifying race for another event or a final round) rather than performance capacity for its own sake. From this point of view, if three athletes are selected for a team, even a small difference between the person who finishes third in the trials and the fourth place finisher is very important, even if the first ten finishers are within tenths of a second of one another.

Most importantly, our study findings reported in this book provide an overview of the complete athlete. We have attempted to understand the physiological, psychological, and emotional components that interface to support the elite athlete as a "whole being." In the following chapters we will explore those aspects of the elite athlete who is competitive, focused, and motivated in the pursuit of perfection in sport.

References

Linder, D. E., Pillow, D. R., & Reno, R. R. (1988, April). *Shrinking jocks: Derogation of athletes who consult a sport psychologist.* Presented at the annual meeting of the Western Psychological Association, San Francisco.

Murphy, S. M., & Ferrante, A. P. (1989). Provision of sport psychology services to the U.S. team at the 1988 Summer Olympic Games. *The Sport Psychologist, 3,* 374–80.

Ogilvie, B. C. (1974, October). Stimulus addiction: The sweet psychic jolt of danger. *Psychology Today,* pp. 88–94.

Ogilvie, B. C. (1979). Critical issues in the application of clinical psychology in the sport setting. *International Journal of Sport Psychology, 10,* (3), 178–83.

Ogilvie, B. C., & Tutko, T. A. (1971, October). If you want to build character, try something else. *Psychology Today,* pp. 61–63.

Raiport, G. (1988, November 18). *New York Times,* p. 22.

Roberts, G. C., & Kimiecik, J. C. (1989). Sport psychology in the German Democratic Republic: An interview with Dr. Gerd Konzag. *The Sport Psychologist, 3,* 72–77.

CHAPTER 2

"Rather than always hoping for the best to happen . . . you must ask yourself what is the scariest or most intimidating part of your race . . . and then visualize it in a positive light. If you have had something awful happen to you, visualize it and change the scenario. You have the power to change the outcome!"

Nancy Ditz
1988 U.S. Olympic Team
Marathon

Mental Practice Among Elite Athletes

Ask someone to describe what a typical training regimen might include for the Olympic track and field athlete and it is almost a given that such things as stopwatches, diets, weights, early morning runs, and fierce competition will come up sooner or later in the conversation. It is less likely that much mention will be made of armchair exercises where athletes are encouraged to sit quietly and visualize their competitive strategies. The image of a Mary Decker Slaney reclining in her easy chair with her eyes closed is unlikely to be the first to pop into one's head when asked to picture what her workouts are like. Obviously the majority of the elite athlete's time spent training is and should be devoted to physical conditioning. However, mental training by elite athletes is on the rise and has received increased attention in sports science circles in recent years. The following is a review of the literature concerning the relationship between mental practice and athletic skill performance. Emphasis is placed on the studies that appear most related to the world of sport, particularly ones which may have direct implications for our research on training of elite track and field athletes.

IMAGERY AND VISUALIZATION
WITHIN MENTAL PRACTICE

In discussing the subject of mental practice in the context of top level athletics, the term "mental imagery" may sound more familiar to some. Although the two are not exactly synonymous, they are very similar. It might be best to consider mental practice a generic term referring to the repetition of a task, without observable movement, with the specific intent of learning. Imagery should then be considered a specific and very common type of mental practice (Suinn, 1985). Imagery has been defined as an exercise using all of the senses in order to create an experience in the mind. This definition also includes imagery as recreating or creating (Vealey, 1986). In regard to the first component, using all the senses, Vealy suggests that, although imagery is often termed visualization, the visual, auditory, olfactory, taste, tactile, and kinesthetic senses are all important.

To illustrate this point Vealey offers the example of a wide receiver in football:

> "The receiver uses his visual sense to read the defense and focus on the ball before catching it. He uses his auditory sense to listen to the snap count barked by the quarterback. He uses his tactile and kinesthetic sense to run his pattern, jump in the air, catch a hard thrown ball, and touch both feet in bounds. He may also smell freshly mown grass and the sweat of his jersey when he is tackled. He may even taste the saltiness of his own sweat."

Utilizing all the senses, an athlete also focuses on the importance of emotions. Imagery can be used to help control anxiety, anger, or pain, and athletes must be able to recreate these emotions in their minds to understand how and why they affect their performance. Imagery as recreating or creating is an important element in the learning process. It has been suggested that some athletes are able to imitate the actions of others (e.g., the serve of a professional tennis player) because their minds "take a picture" of the activity that they use as a model for their performance. Imagery is based on memory, and we experience it internally by reconstructing external events in our mind. As the programmer of our own imagery tapes, we are able to build an image from whatever pieces of memory we choose. We can even use literal photographs to build images, as in this example:

> "Before the 1976 Summer Olympics, representatives from the Soviet Union shot pictures of the Olympic facilities in Montreal. These pictures were returned to the Soviet Union and studied by the athletes. Although the Soviet athletes had not been to Montreal, they used the pictures to create images of themselves performing in those facilities. Creating these types of images served to familiarize the athletes with the Olympic environment before they arrived" (Vealey, 1986).

Possibly the most studied form of mental practice within the sport psychology literature is the form of imagery known as visual motor behavioral rehearsal or VMBR. Suinn (1984; 1985), who developed the technique out of his work with alpine skiers, describes it in the following way:

"The VMBR technique combines relaxation and imagery in a sequence similar to desensitization. However, it differs from desensitization in that relaxation is not used for counterconditioning purposes but to facilitate imagery control, scenes are longer since they include performance sequences, and the scenes tend to emphasize behaviors that involve physical or psychological skills associated with motor performance."

The four main goals of VMBR are: technique enhancement, error analysis and correction, preparation for competition, and efficacy enhancement. As a method of technique enhancement, VMBR may be used at any stage of training to improve performance. Athletes might also use VMBR to analyze and correct errors in a situation where performance is declining and a consultant is hired to guide the athlete in restructuring form or technique. This might occur by analyzing poor technique followed by correction of these bad habits. Once the mental image is corrected, the athlete is then encouraged to implement these changes on the track or field. VMBR can be used to prepare for competition by imagining the details of the competitive situation and the ways in which the athlete will meet its challenges. Athletes may use VMBR to enhance efficacy by imagining themselves performing well and feeling confident as they compete.

Although many studies of mental practice have included athletic activities, relatively few have incorporated elite athletes as subjects. The number of research endeavors involving these populations is increasing; but most of the material available to date is based on the anecdotal accounts of practicing sport psychologists, coaches, and elite athletes themselves. Although these kinds of data may not be a sufficient basis for systematic conclusions, they are interesting and can be a valuable source of information to those directly involved in the training of the elite athlete. One goal of the Elite Athlete Project was to add to the systematic knowledge about mental practice in this unique population.

MENTAL PRACTICE EFFECTIVENESS

The effects of mental practice on motor skill learning and performance have been the subject of over 100 research studies since the 1930s (Feltz & Landers, 1983; Hall, Rodgers & Barr, 1990; Hall, Prongrac & Buckolz, 1985; Mumford & Hall, 1985). The question central to the great bulk of this material has been whether mental practice prior to performing a motor skill will enhance one's performance. Unfortunately, results have been mixed and conclusions contradictory. Whereas some reviewers have found that mental practice appears to enhance motor skill performance (Feltz & Landers, 1983; Richardson, 1967), others have argued that the existing literature offers too few clear-cut answers on which to base any significant conclusions (Corbin, 1972). Feltz and Landers (1983) and others (Paivio, 1985; Rodgers, Hall & Buckolz, 1988) have emphasized the importance of examining the conditions under which mental practice improves task performance. Their analysis of 146 results from sixty studies indicated that mental practice improves performance on cognitive or symbolic tasks more than on motor or strength tasks. However, none of the studies reviewed examined groups of world-class athletes such as those surveyed here in our Elite Athlete Project. It may be that different individual task characteristics are related to more effective mental practice at this very high skill level.

THREE THEORETICAL EXPLANATIONS FOR EFFECTS OF MENTAL PRACTICE

How can a sensory experience in our mind enhance our ability to perform in sport? Feltz and Landers (1983) examined three possible reasons why mental practice may work:

1. the symbolic learning explanation;
2. the psychoneuromuscular explanation;
3. what may be termed the "psyching-up" or motivational explanation.

According to the symbolic learning explanation, rehearsal of the sequence of movements involved in a task is useful because these movements are symbolic components of the task. This explanation implies that the effectiveness of mental practice will be greater when cognitive factors are the primary attributes of the skill being practiced. Feltz and Landers' (1983) analysis is consistent with this hypothesis because it finds that mental practice has much larger effects on cognitive tasks than on tasks characterized as primarily involving motor skills or strength. Although most athletic performance skills probably emphasize motor skills and/or strength, many may involve cognitive, motor, and strength elements to a greater or lesser degree.

The psychoneuromuscular explanation states that mental practice is effective because it produces very small muscle contractions similar to those involved in physical practice. Feltz and Landers' (1983) review of the evidence concerning this theory suggests that it is not a viable explanation of the mechanism by which mental practice may work.

What we term the "psyching-up" or motivational explanation states that in studies of the psychoneuromuscular hypothesis the nonlocalized muscular activity associated with mental practice represents a level of overall arousal which may be optimal for athletic performance. Also, mental practice may facilitate a "set" to perform that actually results in improved performance.

It is possible that mental practice works in different situations for different reasons; for example, the symbolic learning explanation may apply to tasks with a larger motor or strength component. Our goal in the Elite Athlete Project was to examine which elite track and field athletes use how much of which kinds of imagery, with what effect on Olympic team selection.

CHARACTERISTICS OF IMAGERY

The images athletes have during mental practice may be internal or external, visual or kinesthetic, more or less controllable, more or less clear, and associated with strong or weak emotions and physical sensations. Previous researchers have examined some of these components of imagery. For example, perspective of the images may be external or internal. In external imagery, one views from the perspective of an external observer (much as with home movies). Internal imagery, on the other hand, consists of an approximation of the real life experience such that one actually imagines being inside one's own body and experiencing the sensations which might be expected in the actual situation. In a study involving U.S. Olympic gymnasts, Mahoney and Avener (1977) found that all of the male finalists for the 1976 Olympic Team reported using imagery extensively in their preparation for competition. However, the more successful athletes reported a higher frequency of internal rather than external images. Hale (1982) also found internal imagery to be superior to external imagery from a physiological standpoint, and Vealey (1986) argues that an internal perspective may allow for more realistic images than an external perspective.

Imagery Ability and Control

The ability to control one's images is another important element of imagery central to its use in a sporting context. Athletes need to be able to control their imagery consciously if this form of mental practice is to be successful. It is not uncommon for athletes to be plagued by images of themselves failing during competition. Although there is no guarantee that such will be the case during the actual contest, it has been found that the most successful athletes tend to both imagine as well as dream about themselves winning and performing well (Golding & Ungerleider, 1990; Ungerleider, Porter, Golding & Foster, 1989; Mahoney & Avener, 1977). Put in simpler terms, practice makes perfect, if one is practicing the correct response. Practice makes imperfect, if one is practicing the wrong response (Suinn, 1985; Ungerleider, 1985; Ungerleider, Golding, Porter & Foster, 1989). It seems reasonable to hypothesize that this applies as much to mental practice as it does to physical practice.

LITERATURE SUMMARY

Mental practice consists of creating an experience—in this case, athletic performance—in one's mind. A multiplicity of sensations and emotions are involved in mental practice of athletic skills. Images may be internal or external, visual or kinesthetic, more or less controllable, more or less clear, and associated with strong or weak emotions and physical sensations. Theorists speculate that mental practice may work because it facilitates symbolic learning, because it causes small muscular contractions similar to those used in actual sport participation, or because it increases motivation to an optimal level. Evidence on the effectiveness of mental practice is mixed, with some studies suggesting that it depends on the kind of task involved (whether the task primarily involves symbolic, motor, or strength components).

Previous research had not examined mental practice in large numbers of world-class athletes. We wondered how likely elite athletes were to use mental practice strategies, whether some athletes were more likely than others to do so, what the characteristics of athletes' images were, and what the personal meaning of mental practice was for these athletes. We also wondered whether mental practice was related to performance at this world-class level. Survey and interview responses from the Elite Athlete Project allowed us to begin to answer some of these questions. The next section of chapter 2 will deal exclusively with results from our Elite Athlete Project survey.

RESULTS FROM THE ELITE ATHLETE PROJECT

As four-time Olympian and gold medalist Mac Wilkins noted:

> "Basically it boils down to the fact that if you're trying to accomplish something, a particular athletic movement, if you can't visualize it then it's pure chance you will be able to perform the movement. If you visualize it and can really see it . . . you have a clear target to aim for and a much better chance of realizing that target."

We wondered how common such experiences were among the elite athletes we studied. Nearly all of the athletes in our elite track and field study (97%) had heard of imagery, visualization, or mental practice. Almost as many (94%) understood the concept, and 85% (or 524 athletes) practiced some form of it. These results suggest that mental practice is more common among these Olympic hopefuls than among Masters track and field athletes competing in national championships, about 70% of whom reported using these strategies (Ungerleider, Golding, Porter & Foster, 1989).

About one-third of those who reported using some form of mental practice did so once a week or less. About one in five practiced twice a week. Almost another third practiced three to six times a week, and one in ten reported using mental practice more than seven times a week. This pattern differs from that of Masters, who, although they are less likely to use mental practice, when they do use these techniques, use them more often (Ungerleider, Golding, Porter & Foster, 1989). Eighty-three percent used imagery training before their event, almost a third practiced imagery during their event, and a fifth of the sample did this after their event. Using a Likert-type rating scale from 0 (none) to 10 (great amount), we asked athletes to report their total amount of imagery practiced in preparation for their best performance. Median frequency for imagery training was "moderate to great amounts," representing responses of 9 on the scale.

Predictors of Mental Practice Are an athlete's personal characteristics or athletic history related to the likelihood of using mental practice strategies? Older athletes, the more-educated, those who train for more hours each week, those who daydream about their performance, and those who have seen a sports medicine physician in the last two years were more likely than others to report that they use at least some mental practice. Because older athletes tend to be more educated, it is not clear from this analysis whether the older athletes are more likely to visualize because they are older or because they have more education, but we do know that the older, more educated athletes are more likely to visualize.

Track and field athletes were more likely than marathoners to use mental rehearsal strategies. Detailed statistical analyses indicated that if track and field athletes were as old as marathoners, they would be equally likely to use mental practice. Older, more educated athletes may be more likely to use mental practice because their greater experience has shown them it is useful, or because they have had greater exposure to the concept as a result of their education or college coaching, or because their age brings greater patience which facilitates the use of these techniques. In contrast, our study of Masters indicated that *younger* Masters were more likely to use visualization (Ungerleider, Golding, Porter & Foster, 1989). Consistent with our findings among Olympians, that study also indicated that athletes with college competition experience were more likely to use mental practice. Combining these results with the Elite Athlete Project results suggests that mental rehearsal may be most common among athletes in their thirties. It is possible that something about this stage in the life cycle, or growing up during the historical era in which these athletes were raised, predisposes them to the use of visualization.

The relation of training hours to mental practice can have several possible explanations. It is possible that athletes who practice visualization strategies and those who don't practice these techniques do similar amounts of physical training. However, those who use mental practice do so in addition and consider this part of their weekly training and, therefore, report more total hours (mental + physical) as a result. It is also possible that more-committed athletes are more likely both to train more (physically) and to use other methods of enhancing performance, such as mental practice. In this regard, Olympic medalist in two events, Danny Everett told us:

"Just before practice, I do a certain amount of imagery in preparation of that day of workout. That way when I get ready to race, I'm already prepared. The night before competition, I also do imagery and visualization practice so that I can get into the rhythm previously established during my workouts."

The association of treatment by a sports physician with mental practice is somewhat inconsistent statistically, so we should be rather cautious in our interpretation of it. It is possible that the visit to the sports physician suggests the probability of having been injured, and injured athletes use mental practice because they can't practice physically. It is also possible that athletes who seek out this kind of specialist for medical treatment also seek out special cognitive techniques, with both behaviors representing commitment to state-of-the-art training. It is possible that sports physicians influence athletes to use mental practice. In a place like Eugene, Oregon, for example, it is not uncommon to visit any number of top-flight orthopaedic surgeons who offer outstanding medical diagnosis, evaluation, and treatment, as well as alternative strategies for healing injuries. The first author (Steven Ungerleider) had direct experience with an extended healing and recovery process after surgeries for bilateral Achilles tendon ruptures. The rehabilitation and recovery from two surgeries was emotionally and physically debilitating. Fortunately, cross-training exercises like swimming and weight lifting were recommended and encouraged by Dr. Ken Singer, a prominent orthopaedic surgeon and sports medicine professional. Singer, like many other sports-oriented physicians, believes in the emotional healing and recovery process as well as the physiological one.

Both training for long hours and visiting a sports medicine physician may be indicators of commitment to one's athletic career. That daydreaming of competition was also related to mental practice is consistent with this explanation, because people tend to daydream about things that are personally important to them (Singer, 1975). Indeed, athletes in this sample who were more committed to making the Olympic team were more likely to report dreaming of competition (see chapter 3). Consistent with this result, Masters track and field athletes who dreamed about competition were more likely to report using visualization than those who did not report these dreams (Ungerleider, Golding, Porter & Foster, 1989).

Interestingly, whether the athlete worked with a coach was unrelated to whether that athlete used mental rehearsal. Since coaching did not appear to influence use of mental practice strategies, we must wonder where these techniques come from and at what point they are introduced to elite competitors. Clearly, athletes who had previous competitive experience (from high school through postcollege) are more likely to engage in mental practice. This would suggest a coaching influence, but according to our statistical analysis, this finding is not true. Education, however, in addition to athletic experience, did seem to influence the prevalence of mental practice usage. This might suggest that athletes with a college education were more familiar with the sport psychology and physical education literature and perhaps were motivated to seek training manuals and guides from school libraries or institutes. It is also possible that those athletes learned mental practice from former coaches (earlier in their career) and may no longer have or need a coach. Additionally, our data showed that keeping a log of training was also associated with greater mental practice strategies, and therefore may replace the need for daily input from a coach. Thus, athletes who are better educated, more motivated to seek new information, and keep a journal of their own training process, irrespective of their relationship to a coach, might engage in more mental practice activities.

Frequency of Mental Practice Although we knew what some of the characteristics were that were related to whether or not an athlete used mental practice, it was possible that different personal or athletic characteristics were related to how *often* athletes used these techniques, given that they used them at least sometimes. We found that athletes who trained for longer hours were not only more likely to use mental practice, but, among those who did visualize, used these techniques more frequently. Of the three event groups, field athletes visualized most frequently and marathoners least frequently.

Athletes who trained for longer hours also used mental rehearsal techniques more frequently. Training time may be related to frequency of visualization for the same kinds of reasons it is related to whether or not the athlete visualizes. Athletes competing in field events may use mental practice more frequently than those in other events because field events have a large visual component. In fact, many field athletes have commented that it is easier to do imagery and imagery correction when you can stop, visualize the bar, and then set or correct the images before proceeding. Dwight Stones, at the 1984 Olympic Games in Los Angeles, was renowned for "locking in" his images or shaking his head publicly when he didn't "lock in," prior to his approach on the high jump.

Conversely, marathoners may visualize less frequently because endurance and multiple fatigue factors during a race are difficult (and time-consuming) to visualize. Marathoners may have less training time left for visualization after lengthy training runs. Also, as a result of pain and fatigue toward the end of a 26.2 mile race, marathon competitors may be focusing on survival and monitoring pain as opposed to setting up imagery strategies.

We were intrigued by the various strategies athletes use and how much imagery is conducted in preparing for their most important competitions. The only athletic characteristic associated with using more imagery for the athlete's best performance was training time. Across all these measures of imagery, amount of time spent in training appears to be associated with more mental practice. This suggests that the more dedicated, committed athletes will be likely to train longer, perhaps harder, and use cognitive strategies to enhance performance.

Timing of Mental Practice Questions about the timing of mental practice were also included in the questionnaire. When asked whether they use visualization *before* competition, nearly all athletes who use visualization (99%) responded affirmatively. When we asked the athletes whether they engage in mental practice *before* an event, track athletes were more likely than marathoners to report mental practice before the event. More educated athletes, those who dream about competition, and those who daydream about competition were also more likely to report mental practice before their event. This finding might suggest a causal relationship between athletes' obsession with their sport and their daily training which lends itself to daydreaming as well as greater mental practice. The causal direction of this preoccupation might be difficult to establish because one could argue that using lots of mental practice leads to lots of daydreaming about an event or vice versa.

Speaking about a preparation for his best performance ever, 1988 Olympian in the 1,500 meters, Jeff Atkinson, said:

> "My win in the U.S. trials was marked by a very steady and extensive buildup of all aspects of my training—physical as well as mental preparation. I knew my race tactics and what my strategy would be. Those pieces came together in such a way that by the time I got to the start of the race—I was totally certain everything would be okay!"

The fact that track athletes visualize more *before* an event validates our earlier finding about field athletes. Track athletes don't have the time, nor perhaps an adequate strategy, to visualize during an event; thus, it seems they would prefer to visualize before they race.

Visualization *during* competition was less common, with slightly more than one-third of athletes who use visualization reporting this practice. Field athletes were more likely than track

25

athletes or marathoners to state that they visualized during their event. Our statistical analysis indicated that athletes who consult a sport psychologist are indeed more likely to use mental practice techniques, and to use them more frequently. At the same time, working with a sport psychologist is part of a cluster of characteristics including being young, being a field athlete and not a marathoner, and training for long hours. It is these characteristics that seem to be related more fundamentally to visualization. This finding again confirms the belief that use of a sport psychologist should not serve as a "magic bullet" for anyone's training regimen. Clearly, consultation with a professional facilitator should be used as an adjunct to existing training routines in collaboration with coaching staff, not as a replacement.

Self-Monitoring We also asked athletes in our study whether they monitor their "pain zones" or "body signals" during competition. Older athletes, the more educated, marathoners, and those who had seen a sports physician were more likely to say yes. Older athletes may be more likely to self-monitor because they may be more likely to believe they can be injured (they are no longer invulnerable youngsters) and therefore feel a need to be more vigilant about this possibility. Marathoners may be more likely to self-monitor because there is more time for this behavior during their event. Also, coping with pain and fatigue over long hours of running may orient an athlete to a monitoring procedure so that pace and output become constant. The fact that those who have seen a sports medicine physician are more likely to self-monitor suggests that these athletes may be more likely than others to have been injured, and are therefore attending to possible signs of overtraining or further injury. As a result of visiting a sports medicine professional, athletes may have learned monitoring procedures that focus on pain thresholds and other stimuli that might indicate injury risk.

Characteristics of Images To understand more about how one experiences one's images of athletic situations, we also asked athletes about the perspective of their imagery. For example, we asked the respondents if they use imagery to "see" themselves run through a skill. "If so, do you see yourself from the *outside* (as if watching a video screen) or do you experience the skill from the *inside* (as if you are actually inside yourself performing)?" Responses were on a scale with anchors at 0 (inside view), 5 (half-and-half view), and 10 (outside or video view). About a third of our sample saw themselves in their imagery practice from both perspectives or half-and-half. About one-fifth observed from within or an inside view and a similar number of athletes observed from outside or a video view.

Vicki Huber, a 3,000 meter Olympic athlete, commented:

> "Right before a big race, I'll picture myself running and I'll try and put all the other people from the race in my mind. I try to picture every possible situation that I find myself in . . . behind someone, boxed in, being pushed, different positions, laps to go, and of course the final stretch. And I always picture myself winning the race—no matter what! If I picture myself losing, I automatically erase that out of my mind!"

We next examined the clarity of images among our entire elite athlete sample.

Athletes reported that the clarity of their images was personally important to them. Olympic medalist Mac Wilkins commented:

> "Between Montreal, Los Angeles, and Seoul, the difference was clarity of my focus—clarity of my vision or even my ability to visualize what my target was and how to get there. In 1976 (Montreal), it was crystal clear . . . that clarity was not so sharp, however, in Los Angeles . . . and I knew it and it bothered me!"

We analyzed survey data on the clarity of athletes' images to get more information on this issue.

Images tended to be quite clear, with over one-third of the athletes rating the clarity of their images 8, 9, or 10 on a scale of 0 to 10. In contrast, the five categories representing the least clarity (0 through 4) were used by only a little more than one in ten athletes (13%). Greater clarity was reported by younger athletes and those who competed in high school or college, with marathoners reporting less clear images than track or field athletes. No one of these characteristics, which are related to each other, emerged in statistical analyses as accounting for clarity of images.

Images tended to be associated with strong emotions, with close to half the athletes (43%) choosing the highest three categories to describe the strength of the emotions involved. Only one in ten used the lowest four categories (0 through 3). Stronger emotions were reported by younger athletes. Athletes with high school or college competition experience, and those who competed in events other than the marathon, also reported relatively emotion-laden imagery, but statistical analyses indicated that if they were as old as those without such experience and marathoners, respectively, there would have been no experience-based or event-related differences in the strength of emotions associated with images.

One-fourth of the athletes reported that it was "moderately easy" to control the "feeling" involved in mental practice, with over half (59%) reporting moderate to the greatest possible difficulty (0 through 5). Greater control of the feeling was reported by younger athletes, the less-educated, and those who had competed in high school or college, and less control by marathoners.

Controlling the "picture" was perceived as slightly easier than controlling the feeling. Although the "moderate" category was again the most common (20%), slightly fewer than half the athletes used the half of the scale representing greater difficulty (49%), whereas 59% used the range of 0 through 6. Control of the picture was perceived as more difficult by field athletes. This might suggest that field athletes, in addition to possessing other qualities relating to mental practice, are more kinesthetic in their approach and access to these strategies.

Control of imagery may have positive and negative aspects. Earl Bell, a four-time Olympian (1976–1988) and bronze medalist in the 1984 Los Angeles Olympics noted:

"Mental practice requires more than just a quiet place of concentration. It happens at an involuntary level—so that maybe you don't have complete control over yourself. Sometimes images happen best when you're not in control of everything . . . just like pole vaulting—you are not always in control of every jump!"

Olympians vs. Non-Olympians Margaret Groos, the 1988 Olympic marathoner and winner of the U.S. trials, commented:

> "I think my mental preparation for the marathon helps me in my training—usually I imagine certain points in the race; catching someone, pulling away from someone, or the finish of the race. If you haven't done your mental homework in training, then you don't have anything to fall back on."

We next examined whether those who did their "mental homework" were more likely to make the team. Olympians (those who were selected for the U.S. team) and non-Olympians (those who didn't make the U.S. team) were equally likely to have heard of mental practice and to understand this set of techniques. The two groups of athletes were also equally likely to report using mental practice strategies before the Olympic trials. This result suggests that whether or not the athletes used visualization was unrelated to their success at the trials. However, it would be incorrect to conclude that mental practice is *not* helpful, because a large majority of both Olympians and non-Olympians used visualization before the trials.

When mental practice *after* the Olympic trials (in the November 1988 survey) was examined, we found that Olympians were significantly more likely than non-Olympians to use visualization in the period *between the U.S. trials and the Olympic Games in Korea.* This finding suggests that anticipating Olympic participation, and perhaps receiving some additional "booster" training from team coaches and consultants, may have motivated athletes to include more mental practice in their training regimen.

Olympians and non-Olympians tended to be similar in the extent to which they were likely to use mental practice strategies before, during, and after competition, both before and after the Olympic Games. There were two exceptions, both concerning the visualization process during the period between April 1988 and October 1988. Among field athletes, Olympians were more likely than non-Olympians (more than four-fifths compared to about one-half) to visualize during competition. Female Olympians were more likely than female non-Olympians (one-half compared to about one-fifth) to visualize after competition.

Among field athletes, Olympians were more likely than non-Olympians (one-half compared to fewer than one-tenth) to use other forms of mental preparation between April and October 1988. This result is consistent with the pattern of greater involvement in mental practice techniques among Olympians, particularly Olympic *field* athletes, during the period after the trials, when they were preparing for the 1988 games.

Olympic and non-Olympic athletes who used mental practice tended to be similar with respect to the amount of visualization they used. The exception is that, among women, Olympic athletes "saw" themselves compete using mental images more times than did non-Olympians during the period between April and October. When characteristics of images among athletes using mental practice were examined, Olympians reported that their images before the trials had a slightly more external perspective and were associated with stronger physical sensations than did non-Olympians. This finding on external perspective contrasts with past research on Olympic gymnasts where internal imagery was more prevalent among team finalists (Mahoney & Avener, 1977). This suggests the possibility that the consequences of imagery perspective differ depending on the sport in which the athlete participates. Track and field competitors may need to factor in environmental concerns such as weather, crowd and noise level, and artificial surfaces in order to access a complete picture of their success. As Olympic marathoner Nancy Ditz put it:

> "Hot weather is always difficult for me. So visualizing running in hot, humid conditions is an important part of my training. I just visualize it being hot—and not feeling warm. My technique is to image the absolute worst case scenario and then respond positively to it."

The finding on strength of sensations is more intuitive, and suggests that more kinesthetically vivid images may be associated with more effective athletic performance. Kinesthetic imagery has been reported by several athletes who note that after they "see themselves" performing, a strong sense of "physical" strength and competence emerges in their imagery process.

Surprisingly, during the period between the trials and the games, non-Olympians reported greater control than Olympic competitors over both the feeling and the picture involved in their images. This pattern was particularly characteristic of track and marathon athletes. Since nonteam members usually continued the season by competing in Europe and other international venues after the trials, one might interpret this result as suggesting that not being selected for the Olympic team serves as a motivation to increase efforts at imagery control in an attempt to improve performance. Likewise, this strategy may, in fact, not be as powerful a training tool as focused imagery with associated physical sensations.

SUMMARY—IMPLICATIONS AND APPLICATIONS

The primary role of a coach and/or sports consultant is to assist each athlete with reaching his or her peak potential, at least partly by facilitating an ideal psychological state which will allow for the maximum utilization of physical talents. Like most other aspects of the athlete's training, this requires practice—mental practice. Additionally, it may require knowing more of the personal attributes and sensitivities of an athlete. It may be that coaches and staff learn how each athlete accesses imagery, how visual or kinesthetic athletes are, and how powerful images are in the repertoire of the athletic milieu. Since we know that most elite athletes use these techniques, it is very important to STOP, LOOK, AND LISTEN to our competitors and ask how they use and access their mental practice strategies. Several books offer exercises in this process (Harris & Harris, 1984; Orlick, 1988; Porter & Foster, 1986; Williams, 1986). As 1988 Olympian Danny Everett noted:

> "My coach is the most important support system for me now. Our workouts are a product of a relationship between athlete and coach. We have a history of working well together and a special rapport. John and I do mental and physical surgery during our workouts . . . we dissect portions of the race, the start, the first 100, the second, the third, and then the finish. We look at stride, hand motion, and posture. . . . We are very scientific about our approach to racing!"

The fact that Olympians used more visualization than non-Olympians during the period directly after the U.S. trials through the Olympic Games is important and may offer some insight for further research, training development, and intervention. We know that athletes who made the team in July 1988 were very excited and proud of this accomplishment and athletic achievement. We also know that they were now refocusing and preparing for one of the most important competitions of their lives, the Olympic Games, and perhaps a medal to bring home. The motivation and mind-set provided some important goals for which to strive. It is noteworthy, but not extraordinary, that athletes would reach for something special like mental practice, visualization, or alternative supplemental strategies to enhance their physical training during this critical period. Perhaps consultants and national governing body coordinators need to implement imagery training well before the U.S. trials, and perhaps even earlier in the year, so that this process is not rushed or perceived as a last-minute "fix" or "magic bullet" to enhance performance.

Additionally, we were intrigued with our finding that field athletes use significantly more imagery and other forms of mental preparation than others. This suggests that the nature of the event (i.e., jumping, throwing, vaulting) allows for a greater visual component. When preparing for a pole vault, athletes told us that they spend several minutes rehearsing the approach, the pole placement, body thrust, and pole release before they even take off down the runway. The amount of time that field athletes use to prepare for the execution of their event is in sharp contrast to 1,500 meter racers who line up, and immediately face a starter gun signalling their race. Likewise, it is equally difficult for marathoners to maintain imagery focus for two hours while monitoring pain, fatigue, and race strategy. Perhaps more work, including on-site interview and dialogue, needs to occur so that sports consultants can better adapt their mental preparation strategies to the appropriate athletic venue.

It is not uncommon for athletes to recall special moments in their training or competitive races where all the pieces seemed to fit together. As Olympic marathoner Margaret Groos noted:

"I know the minute the gun goes off whether it's going to be my race or not. It's sort of an effortless feeling. You feel that the amount of effort that you're putting out is somehow minimal compared to other races . . . you just float along! It feels like you are not doing anything and the race is taking care of itself. I have that feeling every once in a while in workouts too . . . it's just this psychological thing where I feel very focused!"

References

Corbin, C. B. (1972). Mental practice. In W. P. Morgan (Ed.), *Ergonomic aids and muscular performance.* New York: Academic Press.

Feltz, D. L., & Landers, D. M. (1983). The effects of mental practice on motor skill learning and performance: A meta-analysis. *Journal of Sport Psychology, 5,* 25–57.

Golding, J. M., & Ungerleider, S. (1990). Athletic dreams of Master's track and field competitors. *Journal of Sport Behavior, 13,* 55–72.

Hale, B. D. (1982). The effects of internal and external imagery on muscular and ocular concomitants. *Journal of Sport Psychology, 4,* 379–87.

Hall, C. R., Pongrac, J., & Buckolz, E. (1985). The measurement of imagery ability. *Human Movement Science, 4,* 107–18.

Hall, C. R., Rodgers, W. M., & Barr, K. A. (1990). The use of imagery by athletes in selected sports. *The Sport Psychologist, 4,* 1–10.

Harris, D., & Harris, B. (1984). *The athlete's guide to sports psychology: Mental skills for physical people.* Champaign, IL: Leisure Press.

Mahoney, M. J., & Avener, M. (1977). Psychology of the elite athlete: An exploratory study. *Cognitive Therapy and Research, 1,* 135–41.

Mumford, B., & Hall, C. R. (1985). The effects of internal and external imagery on performing figures in figure skating. *Canadian Journal of Applied Sport Sciences, 10,* 171–77.

Orlick, T. (1986). *Psyching for sport: Mental training for athletes.* Champaign, IL: Leisure Press.

Paivio, A. (1985). Cognitive and motivational functions of imagery in human performance. *Canadian Journal of Applied Sport Sciences, 10,* 22S–28S.

Porter, K., & Foster, J. (1986). *The mental athlete.* Dubuque, IA: Wm. C. Brown.

Richardson, A. (1967). Mental practice: A review and discussion (Part 1). *Research Quarterly, 38,* 95–107.

Rodgers, W., Hall, C. R., & Buckolz, E. (1988). *The effect of an imagery training program on imagery ability, imagery use, and figure skating performance.* Unpublished manuscript, University of Western Ontario, London, Ont.

Singer, J. L. (1975). *The inner world of daydreaming*. New York: Harper Colophon.

Suinn, R. M. (1976, June). Body thinking: Psychology for Olympic champs. *Psychology Today*, pp. 38–44.

Suinn, R. M. (1984). Visual motor behavioral rehearsal: The basic technique. *Scandinavian Journal of Behavior Therapy 13*, 131–42.

Suinn, R. M. (1985). Imagery rehearsal applications to performance enhancement. *The Behavior Therapist, 8*, 155–59.

Ungerleider, S. (1985). Training for the Olympic games with mind and body: Two cases. *Perceptual and Motor Skills, 61*, 1291–94.

Ungerleider, S., & Golding, J. (1988). *An assessment of mental preparation among Masters athletes*. Paper presented at the 1988 Seoul, Korea, Olympic Scientific Congress.

Ungerleider, S., Golding, J. M., Porter, K., & Foster, J. (1989). An exploratory examination of cognitive strategies used by Masters track and field athletes. *The Sport Psychologist, 3*, 245–53.

Ungerleider, S., Porter, K., Golding, J., & Foster, J. (1989). Mental advantages for Masters. *Running Times, 150*, 18–20.

Vealey, R. S. (1986). Imagery training for performance enhancement. In J. M. Williams (Ed.), *Applied sport psychology. Personal growth to peak performance*. Palo Alto: Mayfield Press.

Williams, J. M., (Ed.). (1986). *Applied sport psychology. Personal growth to peak performance*. Palo Alto: Mayfield Press.

CHAPTER 3

"The negative dreams that I had have been during a negative phase in my training, and it obviously means that I didn't have confidence in my training. It's very important to pay attention to this and change your training around so that you feel confident. I think that you should go through this issue with your coach, because the type of workouts and negativity may reflect overtraining. I think that building a winning attitude during workouts, where you feel like you've accomplished something, will help you refocus and get you back to better dreams."

Margaret Groos
1988 U.S. Olympic Team
Marathon

Dreams and Daydreams

The previous chapter examined mental practice, which involves using imagery of athletic activities in a waking, purposeful way. In this chapter we explore the images of athletic activities that occur in dreams and daydreams. In contrast to the logical, structured use of these images in the context of mental practice, dreams and daydreams may be considered *prelogical* forms of thinking (Tauber & Green, 1959). That is, they are less rational, more intuitive, and seem to be more metaphorical, distorted, transformed, and symbolic (Hobson, 1988; Hunt, 1989; Singer, 1984; Tauber & Green, 1959). Dreams and, to a lesser extent, daydreams, are less influenced by our external environment than is ordinary consciousness (Singer, 1984). At the same time, however, dreams and daydreams appear to have continuity with ordinary, day-to-day experience (Singer, 1984). Mahoney and Avener (1977, p. 140) concluded from their research with elite athletes that "sports-related dreams could offer additional information on the psychological functioning of the competitive athlete. The content and frequency of those dreams might provide supplementary information and suggestive guidelines for helping the athlete to focus on specific problem areas. . . . In addition, the fantasies of the athletes—both verbal and visual—may serve a . . . role in athletic counseling and coaching." Before reviewing research on athletes' dreams we will briefly review theoretical approaches to dreaming.

THEORETICAL APPROACHES TO DREAMING

What is a dream? People have wondered about the origins, meanings, and purposes of dreams for many centuries. The ancient Egyptians believed that dreams foretold the future. A series of books listing interpretations of a variety of dreams was written in Egypt in 2000 B.C. (Koulack, 1986). The ancient Greeks, Romans, and Hebrews had similar beliefs about the significance and interpretation of dreams (Cartwright, 1977; Hunt, 1989; Koulack, 1986; Robbins, 1988). Dreams are important in the Bible and in the works of Plato, Aristotle, and Homer (Hunt, 1989; Robbins, 1988). Believing that dreams predict the dreamer's future, members of these cultures—one of which originated the Olympic Games—would expect athletes who dream of winning competitions to win in waking events.

Theoretical approaches to dreaming have been classified as clinical vs. experimental (Cartwright, 1977). Clinical approaches include psychoanalytic and existential theories, whereas experimental approaches focus on cognitive and psychophysiological aspects of dreaming. Within these categories, we will briefly summarize a few illustrative theoretical approaches.

Psychoanalytic Approaches Freud's *The Interpretation of Dreams,* published in 1900, is probably the most influential modern work on dreams. In contrast to the ancient belief that dreams depict what will happen in the future, Freud believed that dreams depict what the dreamer *wishes* would happen. According to Freud, dreams do not depict just any wishes, but specifically deal with wishes that are unacceptable to our waking selves, particularly those related to sexuality (Hunt, 1989; Robbins, 1988). Because these wishes are unacceptable to us, they would disrupt sleep if they became conscious; therefore, the dream disguises the unacceptable wish using symbols, allowing us to remain asleep (Cartwright, 1977; Dallett, 1973; Koulack, 1986; Robbins, 1988).

Because Freudians (and adherents of many other clinical views as well) view dreams as symbolic, the distinction between *manifest* and *latent* content of dreams becomes important (Dallett, 1973; Hunt, 1989; Robbins, 1988). The manifest content refers to what the dream *appears* to be about; for example, a hurdler might dream of jumping over a series of hurdles. The latent content refers to the *meaning* of the dream symbol; for example, a dream of hurdling may represent sexual intercourse. Thus, when we ask athletes whether they dream about practicing, competing, or winning, we are asking about the manifest content of the dream. From a strictly Freudian perspective, these dreams may fundamentally have little to do with athletic competition.

Adler, a neo-Freudian, disagreed with Freud's emphasis on dreams' wishful function and their sexual latent meanings (Robbins, 1988). In contrast, Adler saw dreams' content as representing solutions to problems or resolutions of unfinished daytime business (Cartwright, 1977; Dallett, 1973; Robbins,

1988). Much contemporary research is consistent with this perspective, suggesting that current concerns play an important role in dream content (Singer, 1984). By *current concerns* we mean unfinished business or intentions not acted upon, whether representing long-term, serious conflicts or everyday tasks. For most athletes preparing for the Olympic trials, both the long-term goals of making the team and winning Olympic medals and the shorter-term goals related to practice before the trials represent current concerns.

Because Adler maintained Freud's distinction between the manifest and latent content of dreams (Robbins, 1988), he saw dream solutions as metaphorical (Cartwright, 1977; Robbins, 1988). Thus, from an Adlerian point of view, dreaming of a new way to compete successfully might not represent a literal solution to the problem of more effective technique. According to Adler, the most important thing about dreams is not the solution they present to the problem at hand, but rather, the emotions they evoke in the dreamer—emotions that motivate the dreamer to act in waking life (Cartwright, 1977; Robbins, 1988). Applied to Olympic preparation, this perspective would suggest that dreaming of winning might evoke feelings of joy and confidence that positively affect the athlete's practice and competition.

Like Freud, Jung saw dreams as symbolic (Johnson, 1986). However, in contrast to Freud's view that dream symbolism served to *disguise* inner thoughts or wishes, Jung viewed dream symbolism as serving the interest of *expressing* the dreamer's concerns (Hobson, 1988; Robbins, 1988). To Jung, the dream symbol was the best possible metaphor for the dreamer's situation (Dallett, 1973). Rather than seeing dreams as the product of weakness or neurosis, Jung saw dreams as "clear and undisguised creative expressions of a deep visual-imaginal intelligence" (Hunt, 1986, p. 262).

The Freudian distinction between manifest and latent dream content has a rough parallel in the Jungian distinction between objective and subjective levels (Dallett, 1973). The objective level refers to situations and people in the dreamer's outer life, whereas on the subjective level, dream elements refer to aspects of the dreamer's personality (Dallett, 1973; Johnson, 1986). For example, on the objective level a dream of a shy athlete winning a race against a more gregarious competitor might be about athletic competition. On the subjective level, though, this dream might refer to the dreamer's *internal* shy side "winning out" in their life over their capacity to be gregarious.

Jung saw the main function of dreaming as communication of information from the unconscious that would allow the conscious self to restore inner balance or harmony (Cartwright, 1977; Dallett, 1973; Johnson, 1986; Robbins, 1988). This information frequently takes the form of presentation of the dreamer's unlived possibilities (Dallett, 1973). In an athletic context, an example might be a dream of winning showing the dreamer a more successful or more creative athlete within him or herself of whom he or she had not been consciously aware.

Existential Approaches Gendlin (1986) takes an eclectic approach to dreaming that we classify as existential because of his focus on the primacy of the individual's experience. For example, he tells the reader, "If you don't like this theory, don't let it get in the way of the experiential steps the book describes. . . . You don't need the theory for them" (p. 141). He provides a variety of approaches to understanding dreams which borrow from Jungian and Freudian perspectives, and recommends that readers use any combination of these approaches that enables them to arrive at a breakthrough to understanding the dream. Dream interpretation begins with a "felt sense," a vague "contentless tension" (Hunt, 1989, p. 213) about the dream. Working with various methods to understand the dream results in a "physically felt shift . . . a physically felt release, a bit of energy freed up *in your body*" (Gendlin, 1986, pp. 1–2, emphasis in original). At this point the meaning of the dream is unquestionably clear to the dreamer. Again, this perspective values the individual's deeply felt experience above the particular theoretical model used.

In an athletic context, dreaming about sport participation could have any meaning; the most important thing, from this perspective, is that the meaning feel true to the individual dreamer. One might speculate that the physical sensation involved in understanding dreams might have implications for athletic activity.

Cognitive Approaches Several aspects of traditional cognitive psychology can be seen as having counterparts in dreaming. Dreaming may play a significant role in information processing. During sleep, when there are no new experiences to monitor and remember, the brain can review and reorganize information (Hobson, 1988). REM sleep may be especially useful in facilitating the processing of personally threatening stimuli (McGrath & Cohen, 1978). To the extent that anticipating a major athletic event is personally stressful, this suggests that REM sleep (whether or not the athlete dreams about sports) may help the athlete adjust to this stress. Indeed, there is evidence that incorporating waking stressful experiences into dreams may be associated with *worse* adjustment to the stress (DeKoninck & Koulack, 1975; Koulack, Prevost & DeKoninck, 1985). However, there is also evidence that positive dreams may enhance adaptation to stress (DeKoninck & Koulack, 1975; Koulack et al. 1985), suggesting that dreams of successful athletic performance may aid in coping with the stresses of training and competing.

These possibilities parallel current beliefs about waking mental practice. Practice makes perfect, if one is practicing—or dreaming of—the correct response. Practice makes imperfect, if one is practicing—or dreaming of—the wrong response (Suinn, 1985). More generally, one can speculate that dreaming, particularly dreaming of successful performance, may function as a kind of mental practice conducted on a prelogical level (Golding & Ungerleider, 1990). The athlete is exposed to mental images of the behavior she or he is learning.

Dreams have often been thought to have a problem-solving function, and inventors, scientists, and writers have sometimes credited major innovations to dreams (Cartwright, 1977; Koulack, 1986). From this perspective, dreams of great athletic performances may show the dreamer new ways to compete successfully.

Memory is also an important aspect of dreaming. According to Cartwright (1977, p. 96): "dreaming appears to be followed by improved recall of material appropriate to the active, striving, waking life to come"—aspects of life especially relevant for athletic competition. Memories may also affect the content of dreams. Although people usually forget their dreams, and do not recognize, while dreaming, that memories occurring during

42

dreams are memories, memory makes up at least some part of dream experiences (Hunt, 1989). At the same time, dreamers often have greater access to memory *within* the dream state (Hobson, 1988). Dreams may combine memories with imagination in various ways (Hunt, 1989). In an athletic context, one might speculate that winning athletes are likely to dream of success because they have more memories of success to incorporate into their dreams (Golding & Ungerleider, 1990).

Finally, from the perspective of social cognition, dreams can be seen as reflecting people's conceptions of themselves (Kuiken, 1986). Most adults' dreams include the dreamer's waking self as a character (Kuiken, 1986). Applied to an athletic setting, this perspective suggests that athletes who see themselves as winners, whether from the experience of winning frequently or because of having an optimistic attitude, will be more likely to dream of winning.

Psychophysiological Approaches Nineteenth- and early twentieth-century dream researchers such as Alfred Maury and Mary Arnold-Foster conducted experiments on their own dreams, such as having assistants systematically present specific sensory stimuli to them and then waking them and recording their dreams (Hobson, 1988; Hunt, 1989). However, the event that is generally considered the most important advance in experimental research on dreaming was the discovery, in the 1950s, of rapid-eye-movement, or REM sleep (Cartwright, 1977; Hobson, 1988). As its name suggests, REM sleep is characterized by rapid eye movements; it is also associated with a characteristic pattern of electrical activity of the brain (Hobson, 1988). Human adults spend about one-fourth of the night in REM sleep, which occurs in periods of varying lengths throughout the night. When laboratory subjects were awakened during REM sleep, they usually reported dreaming, whereas during other sleep periods, they were much less likely to report dreaming and more likely to report other kinds of mental activity (Cartwright, 1977).

A psychophysiological finding that may have important implications for athletic dreams involves the role of dream movement.

"Animals and humans both directly act out their dreams if the brain centers of motor inhibition are damaged. . . . During dreaming, motor commands are actually being issued by the cortex but not being enacted" (Hobson, 1988, p. 29).

The brain's sensory centers receive information about these motor commands both in the waking state and during REM sleep when the motor behavior is inhibited (Hobson, 1988). Therefore, when we dream we feel as if we were moving even though we are not.

One might speculate, then, that when athletes jump, throw, or run well in their dreams, they receive the sensory feedback that tells them what this technical excellence feels like. If this were true, athletes who dream of practice or competition would quite literally be practicing, in the sense that, during sleep, their brains issue the motor commands used in their sport. A further speculation would be that this practice might enhance waking performance.

Lucid Dreaming A phenomenon that has received much attention in recent research on dreams is *lucid dreaming,* "in which people are consciously aware that they are dreaming while they are dreaming" (LaBerge & Gackenbach, 1988, p. 1). The recognition of lucid dreams challenges our usual assumptions about the distinctions between sleeping and waking consciousness, implying, in the present context, a greater connection among dreams, daydreams, and mental practice. Another feature of lucid dreams is that dreamers can intentionally control the events of their dreams, during the dreams themselves (Tart, 1988). Objective evidence for the existence of lucid dreams comes from laboratory studies in which dreaming subjects signal to experimenters that they realize they are dreaming, using prearranged signals such as a specific sequence of eye movements, changes in breathing patterns, or other muscle changes (LaBerge, 1988). Research on body movements during lucid dreams suggests that body movements intended in these dreams have corresponding muscle contractions recorded from electrodes attached to the dreamer (Schatzman, Worsley & Fenwick, 1988). The latter finding is consistent with psychophysiological evidence (see above) that neural pathways involved in motor skills are stimulated during dreams. In an athletic context, this might suggest that lucid dreams allow the athlete to practice patterns of muscle contraction.

We can speculate that lucid dreaming may have significance for athletes because *if* dreaming about new techniques, or competition, or successful competition, is associated with improved athletic performance, then lucid dreaming would provide a way to increase the frequency of such performance-enhancing dreams. Lucid dreaming appears to be a learnable skill (LaBerge & Gackenbach, 1988). Thus, if dreaming provides either a special way to enhance performance (for example, trying out new techniques without the possibility of injury), or simply allows extra practice, learning to dream lucidly could provide dream experiences that ultimately lead to enhanced performance. This exciting possibility must await future research.

Research on Athletes' Dreams

To date, only a handful of studies have systematically examined the process, content, or goals of athletes' dreams. The questions most common to these research efforts have been:

1. Is there a relationship between frequency of athletic dreams and performance levels?
2. Does dreaming about success correlate with performance levels?
3. Do dream patterns fluctuate prior to upcoming competition?
4. How do athletes view themselves in their dreams?
5. Do athletes dream mainly about competition or practice, and about past, present, or future events?

We summarize these studies below.

Gymnasts Mahoney and Avener (1977) were the first to examine the dreams of elite athletes systematically. They interviewed twelve male gymnasts, seven of whom were selected for the 1976 U.S. Olympic team. Assessing a variety of cognitive attributes of these athletes, they found that dream frequency was one of the variables most strongly associated with whether the athlete was selected for the team. Positive associations were also found between team selection and degree of success in the athlete's dreams. The successful athletes' dream frequency was less likely to change prior to a meet than was the dream frequency of athletes who were not selected.

Wrestlers and Divers In contrast to Mahoney and Avener's (1977) results, a study of thirty-nine elite Canadian wrestlers and forty-four divers (gender unspecified) found no differences between the dream activity of those who were and were not selected for the Pan-American Games and World Championship teams (Highlen & Bennett, 1983). Wrestlers reported dream frequency "suggesting a low-moderate dream rate." Like the gymnasts, both the wrestlers and divers indicated that their sport-related dreams increased moderately before competition and that the athlete in the dream was most frequently the dreamer. Dreams among the athletes tended to involve competition rather than practice, were moderately realistic and typically future-oriented, and were slightly more often about successful than unsuccessful performance.

Water Polo Players A third study exploring the dreams of athletes involved twenty-one 18- to 23-year-old male college water polo players (Carpinter & Cratty, 1983). Nineteen of the twenty-one athletes reported dreaming about their sport, with the average percent of their dream life being 28%. The majority of the water polo players (nearly four out of five) reported that their dreams of the sport involved positive occurrences. Other people in their dreams most often were the coach and other players. Like Highlen and Bennett (1983), these researchers found that sport-related dreams were more frequent as the season progressed and as higher level and more important competitions were encountered. The type of dream imagery the athlete reported was unrelated to the type of waking skill imagery he reported. Coaches' ranking of athletes' intensity of motivation was unrelated to whether the athlete dreamed about water polo, but those who dreamed about water polo were rated as lower in ability by their coaches. The researchers interpreted this result in the framework of a Freudian-type wish-fulfillment.

Masters Track and Field Athletes We recently completed a study of the athletic dreams of two samples of Masters track and field athletes, 210 who competed in the 1984 National Masters Championships, and 446 participants in the 1987 Championships (Golding and Ungerleider, 1990). Slightly fewer than half the athletes in each sample reported dreaming about athletic competition (42% in 1984 and 45% in 1987). Younger Masters, those who competed in high school or college, those who kept a training log or had higher weekly training mileage or marathon experience, and those who practiced visualization and other forms of mental preparation were more likely to report dreaming about competition. Most of the Masters athletes indicated that their dreams depicted success (92% in the 1984 sample, 88% in the 1987 sample), with men and those practicing mental preparation more likely to report dreams of success. Those who dreamed about competition tended to be more anxious than those who did not. There was a slight tendency for athletes who dreamed about track and field to report faster lifetime personal best times for some events. Also, those who dreamed of success tended to report less depression and faster personal best times.

DAYDREAMING

Experts believe that "your imagination, your capacity to daydream or fantasize, to relive the past or probe the future through pictures in your mind's eye, is one of the greatest resources you have as a human being" (Singer & Switzer, 1980, p. 2). Daydreams may be thought of as a link between mental practice of athletic competition and nocturnal dreams of athletic competition. Like dreams, daydreams are a prelogical form of thinking (Tauber & Green, 1959) which are typically not effortful or intentional. One perspective on this similarity is that "fantasy and dreams are part of a single continuing fantasy process which is subject to certain transformations imposed by physiological and stimulus events. It is unnecessary to sleep in order to generate dream-like ideation" (Klinger, 1971). When we consider the similarity of daydreams to mental practice, mental practice of athletic skills can be seen as a way to use daydreams

47

intentionally to improve one's performance (Singer & Switzer, 1980).

Although many people who never become world-class athletes daydream of athletic success, introspective study suggests that some degree of reality is involved in athletic fantasies. For example, a psychologist who often daydreamed of professional football was a successful player of informal football (Singer, 1966). It has also been noted that a condition necessary for benefiting creatively from daydreaming is that the daydream be at least occasionally relevant to a problem (Klinger, 1971). This suggests that daydreams of athletic performance, which are relevant to the problem of improving one's performance, may have creative benefits in helping the individual solve this problem.

We know of no research that directly addresses athletes' daydreams, whether of athletic competition or other subjects. There is evidence, though, that in general, daydreams frequently involve plans for future actions, and allow exploration of alternative behaviors with a variety of outcomes (Singer, 1975). For athletes, this would include daydreams of topics such as techniques that could be used at the next meet, or strategies for an upcoming race. When personal characteristics related to daydreaming are considered, research suggests that women and men have generally similar patterns of daydreaming (although content may differ), and that frequency of daydreaming peaks in late adolescence (Singer, 1975)—an age group in which many Olympic athletes are found. In the Elite Athlete Project, we explored which athletes daydream about competition and success, and the relation of these daydreams to performance.

LITERATURE SUMMARY

Theories of dreaming suggest some speculations about important possible functions of dreaming about sports participation, from generating emotions that may potentially affect performance, to expressing the athlete's "winning" inner personality, to problem solving and information processing, to practice in issuing neural commands essential for movement. Similarly, daydreaming may be related to overt behavior, possibly by serving a problem-solving function. Considering the rapidly growing interest in cognitive and mental practice strategies to enhance performance, it is surprising that more attention has not been given to the study of dreams, both nocturnal and daydream activity.

The little research that has examined athletes' dreams of sports participation suggests intriguing, if mixed, patterns of results across studies. Athletic dreams tended to have a positive emotional tone, typically depicting successful performance (Carpinter & Cratty, 1983; Golding & Ungerleider, 1990; Highlen & Bennett, 1983). Also, athletes tended to dream more about their sports as they approached competition (Carpinter & Cratty, 1983; Highlen & Bennett, 1983), yet the relationship between dream frequency and performance was not consistent. Among gymnasts (Mahoney & Avener, 1977), and possibly Masters track and field athletes (Golding & Ungerleider, 1990), dream frequency was positively correlated with high performance. With water polo players, however, those who dreamed of their sport the most were rated lower in ability by their coaches (Carpinter & Cratty, 1983), and among wrestlers and divers, dreaming was unrelated to performance (Highlen & Bennett, 1983). Many comparisons across studies were not possible because researchers asked different questions or reported their results in different ways.

RESULTS FROM THE ELITE ATHLETE PROJECT

We asked athletes whether they dream about *participation* in their event (whether in the context of practice, competition, or even recreation) and whether they dream about *competition*. Dreams about competition were common, occurring in nearly four-fifths of the athletes. Vicki Huber, the 3,000 meter specialist, remembered some competitive dreams this way:

> "Sometimes before a cross-country race, I would dream about the race for a long time. It's just like I'm running in my dreams and there's not really an end. And my whole night would be like one long race, and I'd wake up exhausted. Not that I wanted to or anything, but it would just happen."

Dreams of competition were much more common in this sample of Olympic hopefuls than in the Masters track and field athletes we studied previously. In that study, slightly fewer than half the athletes reported dreaming about competition (Golding & Ungerleider, 1990). The difference between Olympic and Masters athletes was not surprising for two reasons. In our Masters study, we found that younger athletes were more likely to report dreaming, and younger people dream more in general than do older people (Cartwright, 1977). We know that Olympic hopefuls (with an average age of about twenty-six) are much younger than the Masters (whose average age was fifty). Secondly, if dreams are part of a process of dealing with un-finished business and current concerns, on the average, Olympic hopefuls probably have more invested in the emotional process of their quest for team selection than Masters, who probably tend to have more salient occupational and family concerns. Therefore, the trials participants may be driven to more active and prolific dreams about this important event.

Dreams of any participation were only slightly more com-mon than dreams of competition, being reported by over four-fifths of the athletes. This finding suggests that most of the athletes who dreamed about any participation had at least some dreams of competitive situations. However, dreams of practice were personally significant to athletes who reported them. Olympic medalist Danny Everett told us:

> "Right before the finals of the 400 meters in Seoul, I didn't sleep well. I don't remember dreaming of a race or of a winning experience. I dreamt more of my preparation and training for the race. I seem to place more value on hard work and thorough training than just winning a race . . . maybe that's why it shows up in my dreams as just prepar-ing to race. For me, better preparation equals better confidence."

We wondered which athletes were most likely to dream about track and field participation. Athletes in the Olympic trials sample who trained for longer hours were more likely to report dreaming of both any participation (including practice) and competition. This finding is similar to our finding in the Masters study that athletes who ran more miles each week were more likely to dream about competition (Golding & Ungerleider,

1990). This seems to be consistent with the hypothesis that the more athletes put into their work, the more conscious and unconscious time is spent participating in the event.

We also found that women were more likely than men to tell us that they dreamed about participation. We wondered if this finding would be true if training hours were considered, since our findings suggest that hours of training is related to dreams (and women were more likely than men to be marathoners, who train for long hours because of the nature of their sport). When we controlled training hours statistically, the relationship of gender to amount of dreaming was not consistent. This relationship was limited to the athletes who trained twenty hours or more a week (25% of the sample). This may suggest that in general women and men tend to report or remember their dreams equally often, but among the athletes who train the hardest, women are more likely than men to report dreaming activity, whether because they are more likely to dream of their event or because they are more likely to recall these dreams.

Frequency of Dreams We asked athletes who reported dreaming about track and field how often they had these dreams. Although athletic dreams were common, they occurred fairly infrequently, with about one-third of the athletes in our study who dreamed about participation or competition reporting these dreams less than once a month. More than another third of the sample reported dreams once or twice a month. Most of the remaining third of the sample reported dreaming once to a couple of times a week, with a small number of athletes (nineteen) dreaming of participation or competition every night. It seems reasonable to expect that athletes who remember dreams about any topic more frequently are more likely to remember dreams about athletic topics. PattiSue Plumer, a 3,000 meter Olympian, told us:

> "I never finish the race in my dreams . . . I don't think. I can't remember—maybe I have, but it doesn't stand out in my mind. It's usually like flashes. I dream a lot in general and I'm a person that every night has a lot of different dreams, but I don't remember dreaming and winning a race in my dreams."

We wondered which athletes would dream most frequently about their track and field participation. Younger, unmarried athletes and those who had competed in high school or college were likely to report dreaming more often about both participation and competition. Both kinds of dreams were most frequent among field athletes and least frequent among marathoners.

Athletes who worked with a coach also dreamed more frequently of competition. We wondered whether working with a coach was related to frequent competitive dreams because it reflected athletes' commitment to making the team. To investigate this possibility, we examined the relationships of dream frequency with self-reported commitment to making the team and with perceiving the sacrifices made to train for the trials as stressful. Athletes who reported high levels of commitment to making the Olympic team and those who had made the most stressful sacrifices to prepare for the trials dreamed more frequently of participation and competition in their event. These findings are consistent with our belief that athletes who put their studies on hold and their business opportunities and personal commitment to family on the back burner had, indeed, made major sacrifices in preparing for the U.S. Olympic trials. This type of all-or-nothing commitment to being an Olympic athlete would certainly preoccupy one's waking and sleeping hours. These athletes "eat, sleep, and breathe" trials preparation in quite a literal sense: they "sleep" it by dreaming about it.

Dreams of Success In further survey questions, we asked the trials participants how often their dreams depicted success. Responses were given on a scale of 0 (never) through 10 (always or almost always). Athletes were about evenly split on this question, with half choosing ratings of 6 or less. One-fourth of those who dreamed about competition gave the response "sometimes." Younger, less-educated, male, unmarried athletes with high school or college experience reported more frequent success in their dream competitions. This finding was similar to our findings among Masters athletes, in which men and former high school athletes were more likely to report dreams of success (Golding & Ungerleider, 1990).

Field athletes reported the most frequent success in dreams and marathoners the least frequent. This finding may be related to results in our earlier chapter on mental practice. Field athletes were consistently more involved with imagery and visualization before and during their field events than track or marathon athletes. If we take the position that mental practice and rehearsal occurs both on the conscious waking level as well as during unconscious sleeping time (Cartwright, 1977), the associations of mental practice and success in dream competitions with competition in field events seem to follow a logical continuum. That is, field athletes report both a high probability and frequency of visualization and a high frequency of success in their dreams of competition.

We also found that a high degree of commitment to making the team was reliably related to dreaming often of success. In spite of differences in age, type of event, education level, and gender, our most detailed analyses indicated that being committed to making the team was most consistently related to frequent dreams of success. Thus, to a point, age, gender, education, and track, field, or marathon participation, do relate to the frequency with which athletes dream of success. However, all things being equal, commitment to making the team and the intense sacrifice of getting there is the best predictor of success in dreams. This finding might suggest that more work be explored by interpreting and debriefing dreams with a coach, trainer, or sports consultant (Mahoney & Avener, 1977). If we are to believe that dreams offer insight and the persistent message of mental preparation, perhaps some additional time during the training process could usefully be devoted to dream exploration.

Daydreams among Elite Athletes Along with nocturnal dreaming, our research also explored daydreaming. Nearly all athletes in our sample reported daydreaming about athletic performance. Younger athletes and those more committed to making the team were more likely to report daydreaming. More detailed analysis, however, suggested that commitment to making the U.S. Olympic team was related to daydreaming about track and field only in the oldest group (top quarter) of athletes in our study. These athletes fell into a range of twenty-nine to forty-five years of age.

Across the board, our younger athletes appeared to be more frequent and prolific dreamers and daydreamers in terms of participation, competition, and success in dreams. However, when controlling for age, it seems that the overriding factor is not age, experience, or education; but in fact, being deeply committed to making the Olympic team and perceiving oneself as experiencing stress and sacrifice in obtaining that goal.

Success in Daydreams We also asked athletes about their success in competitions in their daydreams. Nearly one-third of the athletes reported successful daydreams "always or almost always". Half chose one of the top two frequency categories, and only twenty-four athletes daydreamed of success in their events less often than "sometimes." Like successful dreams, successful daydreams were more likely to be reported by men and competitors more committed to making the Olympic team. The relation of commitment to making the team and daydream success occurred in both men and women. However, the relationship of gender to daydream success depended on level of commitment. Only at moderate levels of commitment was gender related to daydreaming of success. Among the most- and least-committed athletes, gender was unrelated to success in daydreams. Once again, this finding suggests that gender is not the main issue in daydreams. Our findings consistently focus on the issue of personal sacrifice, commitment, and perceiving one's athletic endeavor as a full-time, all-encompassing, and stressful career.

In this study neither dreaming about participation or competition, nor frequency of, nor success in, dreams nor daydreaming was related to whether the athlete made the Olympic team. However, given the complexity involved in dream reporting (see below) and the simplicity of the measure we used, this result does not mean that sports-related dreams are unrelated to athletic success. Clearly, in individual cases dream performance is sometimes related to waking performance. For example, Olympian Margaret Groos told us:

"I dreamt that I made the Olympic team before the trials, and I did. It was probably two weeks before the trials. It really wasn't connected to any one workout, but I just dreamt that I made the team. And it was such a very overwhelmingly positive dream. I mean, I went through the whole thing, the whole race, the whole strategy in my dream, and I won. And I made the team, and the whole elation of making the team, and telling everyone, and it was very detailed and vivid and specific. When I woke up, I had a very, very, positive feeling that I was going to win."

She also reported the opposite experience:

"I've also dreamt that I've done badly in a race and I have. But they always come true; the power of both the positive or negative. In '84, I dreamt the night before the trials that I finished fifth, and I did finish fifth. I vividly remember crossing the finish line, there were four people ahead of me, and they told me I was fifth, and I woke up that morning and I told my friend that I was rooming with, I said, 'Cynthia, I had a dream that I finished fifth.' She said 'Oh, don't worry about that. You'll make the team.' And sure enough, I finished fifth."

SUMMARY—IMPLICATIONS AND APPLICATIONS

Research conducted in the field of sport psychology has risen sharply over recent years. The study of human potential has been expanded to looking at the broad spectrum of human performance. Yet, to date, only a handful of studies have systematically examined the process, content, and goals of athletes' dreams or daydreams.

Clearly, not enough data have been collected on the dream life of athletes to draw any conclusions concerning the effects of dreams on performance. The notion of dreams as a form of mental practice is appealing. However, dreaming is a complex phenomenon which serves various psychological functions (Cartwright, 1977; Hobson, 1988; Hunt, 1989). According to Cartwright (1977), people dream about personal and emotional events, with dream associations being more emotional than logical. Consistent with this perspective, Jeff Atkinson, a 1,500 meter runner on the 1988 Olympic team, told us:

"My dreams don't really focus on winning . . . they are more feeling oriented. I dream more in emotions than pictures. These feelings could be a big win or even a big loss. Sometimes I wake with a feeling of tremendous success—and I have this really supreme feeling all over!"

55

This type of dream would seem to suggest that if athletic dreams do function as a type of mental practice, they mainly act as a means of improving mental toughness, ability to control one's emotional behavior during competitive situations, and coping strategies, rather than improving specific technical skills. On the other hand, from cognitive and physiological perspectives, dreams may organize information relevant to skill development, or may be a way to practice the neurologic behaviors necessary to motor performance. Thus, it is possible that dreaming could serve both emotional and technical kinds of purposes.

Future research on athletes' dreams must address the fact that most dreams are forgotten (Cartwright, 1977). It must also be acknowledged that the survey-type measures of dreaming used in studies of athletic dreams cannot examine comprehensively the complex nature of a subject's sports-related dreams, although they provide useful preliminary information. Much more work is needed in this area before any questions can be answered regarding what impact these kinds of dreams might have on the athlete's life. Considering the emphasis that has been placed on dreams throughout the history of psychology, and the wealth of knowledge that has been accumulated concerning their various properties, functions, and means of measurement and interpretation, it seems important to begin examining this neglected source of information in an attempt to understand better the mental activities of the athlete.

References

Carpinter, P. J., & Cratty, B. J. (1983). Mental activity, dreams, and performance in team sport athletes. *International Journal of Sport Psychology, 14*, 186–97.
Cartwright, R. D. (1977). *Night life: Explorations in dreaming.* Englewood Cliffs, N.J.: Prentice-Hall.
Dallett, J. (1973). Theories of dream function. *Psychological Bulletin, 79*, 408–16.
DeKoninck, J. M., & Koulack, D. (1975). Dream content and adaptation to a stressful situation. *Journal of Abnormal Psychology, 84*, 250–60.

Freud, S. (1965). *The interpretation of dreams*. New York: Avon. (Original work published 1900.)

Gendlin, E. T. (1986). *Let your body interpret your dreams*. Wilmette, IL: Chiron Publications.

Golding, J. M., & Ungerleider, S. (1990). Athletic dreams of Masters track and field competitors. *Journal of Sport Behavior, 13*, 55–72.

Highlen, P. S., & Bennett, B. B. (1983). Elite divers and wrestlers: A comparison between open- and closed-skill athletes. *Journal of Sport Psychology, 5*, 390–409.

Hobson, J. A. (1988). *The dreaming brain*. New York: Basic Books.

Hunt, H. T. (1986). Toward a cognitive psychology of dreams. In J. Gackenbach (Ed.), *Sleep and dreams: A sourcebook* (pp. 251–81). New York: Garland.

Hunt, H. T. (1989). *The multiplicity of dreams: Memory, imagination, and consciousness*. New Haven: Yale University Press.

Johnson, R. A. (1986). *Inner work: Using dreams and active imagination for personal growth*. San Francisco: Harper & Row.

Klinger, E. (1971). *Structure and functions of fantasy*. New York: Wiley.

Koulack, D. (1986). Effects of presleep and during-sleep stimuli on the content of dreams. In J. Gackenbach (Ed.), *Sleep and dreams: A sourcebook* (pp. 207–24). New York: Garland.

Koulack, D., Prevost, F., & DeKoninck, J. (1985). Sleep, dreaming, and adaptation to a stressful intellectual activity. *Sleep, 8*, 244–53.

Kuiken, D. (1986). Dreams and self-knowledge. In J. Gackenbach (Ed.), *Sleep and dreams: A sourcebook* (pp. 225–50). New York: Garland.

Laberge, S. (1988). The psychophysiology of lucid dreaming. In J. Gackenbach & S. LaBerge (Eds.), *Conscious mind, sleeping brain: Perspectives on lucid dreaming* (pp. 135–53). New York: Plenum.

Laberge, S., & Gackenbach, J. (1988). Introduction. In J. Gackenbach & S. LaBerge (Eds.), *Conscious mind, sleeping brain: Perspectives on lucid dreaming* (pp. 1–8). New York: Plenum.

Mahoney, M. J., & Avener, M. (1977). Psychology of the elite athlete: An exploratory study. *Cognitive Therapy and Research, 1*, 135–41.

McGrath, M. J., & Cohen, D. B. (1978). REM sleep facilitation of adaptive waking behavior: A review of the literature. *Psychological Bulletin, 85*, 24–57.

Robbins, P. R. (1988). *The psychology of dreams*. Jefferson, NC: McFarland.

Schatzman, M., Worsley, A., & Fenwick, P. (1988). Correspondence during lucid dreams between dreamed and actual events. In J. Gackenbach & S. LaBerge (Eds.), *Conscious mind, sleeping brain: Perspectives on lucid dreaming* (pp. 155–79). New York: Plenum.

Singer, J. L. (1966). *Daydreaming: An introduction to the experimental study of inner experience*. New York: Random House.

Singer, J. L. (1975). *The inner world of daydreaming*. New York: Harper Colophon.

Singer, J. L. (1984). *The human personality*. San Diego: Harcourt Brace Jovanovich.

Singer, J. L., & Switzer, E. (1980). *Mind-play: The creative uses of fantasy.* Englewood Cliffs, NJ: Prentice-Hall.

Suinn, R. M. (1985). Imagery rehearsal applications to performance enhancement. *The Behavior Therapist, 8,* 155–59.

Tart, C. T. (1988). From spontaneous event to lucidity: A review of attempts to consciously control nocturnal dreaming. In J. Gackenbach & S. LaBerge (Eds.), *Conscious mind, sleeping brain: Perspectives on lucid dreaming* (pp. 67–103). New York: Plenum.

Tauber, E. S., & Green, M. R. (1959). *Prelogical experience: An inquiry into dreams and other creative processes.* New York: Basic Books.

CHAPTER 4

"I found out just maybe a year ago talking to my uncle, that when he was a kid, my granddad used to take my mom running every morning, and I was quite surprised! Because I thought women usually didn't run, you know, back in the 1940s. And he said she used to run at least five miles every morning. Just for health, not competitive or anything. They would wake up in the morning and do five miles, and then on weekends they would go and climb mountains. Maybe that's where my strength, endurance, and motivation comes from! I am still surprised because I always thought my athleticism came from my dad."

Carmen Troncoso
1988 U.S. Olympic Team
10,000 Meters (exhibition event)

Understanding Mood and the Athletic Profile

In recent years a number of books have been written about the health benefits of running and other rigorous exercise. The scientific evidence suggests a connection among physical exercise, mood, and cognitive functioning (Lichtman & Poser, 1983). Additional research has attributed positive mood shift and decreases in anxiety and depression to long distance running (Markoff, Ryan & Young 1982). Research suggests that psychological benefits of exercise include improvements in mood, self-concept, work behavior, and, possibly, cognitive functioning (Dishman, 1985; Folkins & Sime, 1981; Taylor, Sallis, & Needle, 1985), although much of the scientific evidence is mixed and suffers from methodological limitations (Folkins & Sime, 1981; Hughes, 1984; Taylor et al. 1985).

Three recent surveys of general population samples suggest that exercise is associated with low levels of depressed and anxious moods and of malaise (Agnew & Levin, 1987; Farmer et al. 1988; Ross & Hayes, 1988). In the first study, which involved 1,900 adults in a national sample, low levels of both recreational and nonrecreational physical activity were associated with depressed mood (Farmer et al. 1988). People who reported little recreational physical activity at the first interview were more likely to report depressed mood when they were interviewed again eight years later. The second study, which sampled 401 Illinois adults, found that sports participation was related to psychological well-being, measured by using items reflecting depression, anxiety, and general malaise (Ross & Hayes, 1988). Part of this relationship was due to the fact that participating in sports was associated with perceiving oneself as healthier, which was in turn associated with greater well-being. In the third study, which used a national sample of 2,436 adults, exercise participants reported more favorable mood and better self-perceived health than non-exercisers (Agnew & Levin, 1987), although when respondents were interviewed a year later, initial exercise was less consistently related to later mood. However, exercise was consistently related to self-perceived health for many people.

Taken together, these survey studies demonstrate a reliable association between exercise and positive moods. They also suggest that self-perceptions of health may play a role in this association. The main strength of this kind of research is that it allows us to draw conclusions about the relation of exercise and mood in naturally occurring settings in the general population. The longitudinal designs used in these surveys (Agnew & Levin, 1987; Farmer et al. 1988) are especially useful because they allow assessment of whether exercise at an earlier time is related to mood at a later time.

Other researchers have examined moods in athlete populations. In 1977, Morgan and Pollock found that successful athletes tend to differ psychologically from unsuccessful athletes based on a mood profile known as the POMS or Profile of Mood States (McNair, Lorr & Droppleman, 1971). The profile measures six transitory affective states:

1. anxiety,
2. depression,
3. anger,
4. vigor,
5. fatigue,
6. confusion.

The mood profile uses sixty-five adjectives rated on a five-point scale ranging from "not at all" to "extremely." Morgan (1980) coined the phrase "iceberg profile" to describe a pattern characterized by high scores on vigor and low scores on anxiety, depression, anger, fatigue, and confusion. This iceberg profile was more common among the more successful athletes. In two studies involving nonelite track and field athletes, Gondola and Tuckman (1982) administered the POMS to 348 marathoners and compared their results to a normative population of 856 college students. They found that male and female marathoners were significantly less anxious, less fatigued, less depressed, less confused, and more vigorous than male and female college students. Ungerleider and Golding (1989) found that 587 men and women Masters track and field athletes had profiles that were "healthier" than the average college sample and were less depressed, less angry, and less fatigued than nonelite athlete comparison groups.

Using a mood state profile such as the POMS has some implications for all athletes, including track and field competitors. Most coaches and trainers can only second-guess their athletes' level of intensity. They might sit quietly and interview their team members and ask individual athletes how they feel today or how their workouts are going. This is a subjective, and some-times unreliable, procedure in many cases. The best responses might come from athletes who really know their peaks and val-leys, in which case the information is usually helpful. With a diagnostic tool such as the POMS, used in conjunction with a sports consultant, more can be learned about the team and its individual members.

BACKGROUND OF THE POMS

Although the POMS was originally designed as a means of evaluat-ing psychotherapy effectiveness, its use has spread to a variety of settings including sports research. According to LeUnes, Hayward, and Daiss (1989) the POMS has been cited in fifty-six sports-related published papers reporting on nineteen different sports since its introduction to sports in 1975. Although several of these studies will be discussed, this review will concentrate on those involving elite athletes, those at the Olympic and/or professional levels.

Wrestlers

Nagle and his research team (1975) were the first to use the POMS in a sporting context. This initial study involved forty can-didates for the 1972 Olympic freestyle wrestling team. Each can-didate was administered the POMS prior to the selection process. Wrestlers who made the team were compared to those who did not, and all the wrestlers were compared to a general population sample. Nagle and his colleagues found that elite wrestlers were less anxious, depressed, confused, and fatigued, and somewhat more vigorous than the general population. The date also showed that the wrestlers who were chosen for the team were less anxious, less confused, and more vigorous than those candidates who were not selected. Attempts to repeat these findings with elite wrestlers have proved successful, with similar differences in mood being found between candidates qualifying for the 1980 U.S. Greco-Roman and freestyle Olympic wrestling teams (Silva et al. 1985), and in qualifiers vs. non-qualifiers for the 1979 U.S. junior world wrestling team. Similar results were also found in a study of seventy-three members of the U.S. Alpine ski team, which used a different measure of depression (May et al. 1985). Depression was found to be a strikingly significant factor in terms of skier performance, and being depressed at the beginning of the season greatly increased the risk of being dropped from the team. Depressed athletes were cut at a rate of 50% compared to 21% for nondepressed teammates.

Crew and Rowing Athletes

Researchers have continued to use the POMS in assessing the moods of elite athletes in a variety of settings and found the iceberg profile to be a common occurrence among those who have reached the pinnacle of their sport. In studying the moods of top-level crew athletes, Morgan and Johnson (1978) produced data quite consistent with the iceberg profiles found in the previously mentioned elite wrestler study. Fifty-seven U.S. heavyweight rowing team candidates were given the POMS prior to the selection of the sixteen-person squad. Data from these fifty-seven candidates and lightweight crew athletes were compared with a normal college sample. The rowers scored lower on depression and confusion and higher on vigor than did the nonrowing college group. Comparisons between the heavyweight and lightweight crew members produced few significant mood differences, as did comparisons between the sixteen candidates making the U.S. heavyweight team and the forty-one who did not. Thus, in this case, a difference was found between POMS scores of athletes and nonathletes, but not between more successful elite and less successful elite athletes. Similar results have been presented in a study involving a small number of America's best cyclists (Hagberg et al. 1979), and in a comparison between elite sailors and runners (Joesting, 1981).

Track and Field Athletes

Morgan and Pollock (1977), in a highly detailed look into the psychological characteristics of elite distance runners, administered the POMS to marathoners and middle distance runners ranging in ability level from top collegiate competitors to those of world class caliber. These data were compared to the results of Morgan's earlier work with wrestlers and crew athletes and to a general population sample. Whereas the entire athlete sample differed from the general population sample on all POMS mood states except anger, no significant differences were found among the runners at varying levels, or between the runners and the athletes from the two other sports. This result suggests that the iceberg profile characterizes athletes in general rather than athletes in one sport or one type of sport.

Speed Skaters

Male contenders for the 1980 U.S. Olympic speed skating team were another group of top athletes whose moods were measured with the POMS prior to team selection (Gutman et al. 1984). Eleven skaters competing for five spots on the team were administered the POMS six months before the 1979 Olympic winter trials (June), at the end of their summer training (October), and immediately before and after the trials. As was expected, Gutman and his colleagues found that the group as a whole demonstrated the iceberg profile at the initial testing six months prior to the trials. However, those not selected reported more fluctuation of mood, with lower levels of vigor, just prior to the trials. At the time of the first POMS testing, the nonqualifying group had a more pronounced iceberg profile with somewhat higher scores on vigor than the five skaters who were selected for the team. This trend was reversed after the highly intensive training period over the summer. The nonqualifying group showed a significant drop in vigor and increase in fatigue, while the qualifiers increased in vigor and decreased in depression and confusion. Just before the trials in December, all of the skaters showed an increase in vigor and a decrease in fatigue. However, the nonqualifiers did not recover to pretraining levels of vigor, while the qualifiers reported their highest vigor levels of the entire six-month period. Immediately after the trials all skaters showed a marked increase in fatigue and loss of vigor.

Swimmers

One recent application of the POMS has been to identify the onset of staleness in competitive athletes. In a ten-year study of male and female varsity swimmers at the University of Wisconsin, Morgan and his research team (1987) administered the POMS to 400 swimmers at various times throughout the swim season. Defining staleness as "a state characterized by reduced performance with an inability to train at customary levels," the research sought to gain more insight into what causes staleness, and how it can best be detected and thus prevented. By using the POMS to monitor individuals' moods across various time periods in different types of training cycles, the research team concluded that such practices offer considerable potential for the prevention of staleness. The psychological mood state of swimmers seemed to shift from high vigor or the iceberg profile to an inverted position suggesting sluggishness or low vigor as the season progressed. This research suggested that swimmers who were maintaining high-level training routines late in the season were becoming stale. As swimmers began to taper their workouts, the familiar iceberg profile seemed to return.

Whereas overtraining is a technique used in many sports to increase performance, overtraining in conjunction with tapering, or reducing training levels prior to competition, is a standard procedure used by swim coaches to maximize both physical and psychological performance in their athletes. This type of regimen, although effective, makes swimmers quite vulnerable to staleness. Therefore, finding an ideal level of overtraining for each individual is a difficult task. The results of the Morgan study indicated that mood disturbances increased as the training levels increased, and fell to baseline levels with reduction of the training load. Over the ten-year study, it was observed that the greatest amount of mood disturbance occurred in late January following the most intense part of the training period involving the most yards per day. The data showed that during this peak training load it was not uncommon for 5–10% of the swimmers to experience staleness. The researchers reported that during this period they routinely referred athletes with "a staleness profile" to university counseling services where approximately 80% of these individuals were diagnosed as suffering from clinical depression. Reduced levels of vigor and increases in fatigue were the most noticeable changes in mood among the swimmers during periods of overtraining.

Monitoring mood shifts as an indicator of overtraining and fatigue may be a safer and more reliable way of assisting our coaches and athletes in the prevention of stale performances and burnout. This type of mood monitoring has clear implications for all sports, including track and field.

LITERATURE SUMMARY

The studies discussed up to this point have dealt directly with elite athletes, comparing POMS scores of more successful elite athletes to those of their less successful counterparts, and scores of elite athletes vs. general nonathletic populations. Results from the different studies comparing the mood profiles of elite athletes to nonathletic samples have all demonstrated that elite athletes tend to exhibit the iceberg profile quite regularly, while the profile is less often seen in nonathletes. Comparisons of the POMS data from elites of different sports have offered no significant differences in the degree of iceberg effect. The best athletes tend to have very similar mood profiles regardless of type of sport. Within a sport, comparisons among elites have offered mixed results. In the case of elite wrestlers and speed skaters, those who outperformed their competitors demonstrated significantly more noticeable iceberg effects. However, this was not the case with crew athletes and cyclists. In the studies comparing POMS scores of elites and nonelites in the same sport, no significant differences were found in marathoners or middle distance runners. Therefore, it appears that athletes in general exhibit the iceberg profile frequently relative to nonathletes, yet differences within athletic populations are less dramatic and more difficult to use as a base for generalizations.

It appears from the research literature that athletic activity may enhance mood. However, no clear relationship between level of athletic involvement and desirable mood profiles exists. Results are mixed as to whether elite athletes' moods are superior to those of athletes not competing at world class levels. Because most of those engaged in sports activities demonstrate iceberg profiles, attempts to screen or select athletes for certain activities or team positions using the POMS should be carefully complemented with other types of criteria unrelated to mood. As noted in the swimming research, assessing mood shifts during different periods of a long training season may offer clues as to how athletes cope with the intensity of their workouts. Clearly, overtraining and fatigue have severe consequences, including injury and slow recovery to original training schedules. If an instrument such as the POMS, in collaboration with a trained consultant, can assist with monitoring fatigue, depression, and energy levels of elite competitors, greater emphasis might be focused on the quality of training and not quantity of sessions.

This research literature made us curious about whether the athletes we studied would show the iceberg profile seen in past studies of athletes. We also wondered whether athletes' personal or athletic characteristics were related to their mood states, whether Olympians' moods differed from the moods of elite athletes not selected for the team both before and after the selection process, and how these elite competitors' moods changed over time. Thus, the remainder of this chapter is devoted to a discussion of the results from the Elite Athlete Project.

RESULTS FROM THE ELITE ATHLETE PROJECT

Olympian Vicki Huber, the 3,000 meter specialist, spoke candidly about the effect of mood swings:

> "The biggest thing I've been through is post-Olympic depression. I had so much excitement, so much adrenaline for so long, and then it was all over, I didn't know what to do. I didn't know how to handle it. And I was really depressed. It was hard to get up in the morning, and I had no motivation. I was afraid that I wasn't going to run that fast again, you know, it was like a once in a lifetime thing."

We wanted to examine mood states, including depression, especially in the months leading up to the trials.

We used data from the Elite Athlete Project to examine whether personal differences among the athletes were associated with changes in their mood scores. Male and female athletes reported similar levels of all the moods we measured. Younger athletes were more anxious, depressed, angry, and confused than their older counterparts. Athletes who had not graduated from college were also more anxious, depressed, angry, and confused than those who had at least a college education. In addition, the less-educated athletes had greater overall mood disturbance. Similarly, unmarried athletes had greater overall mood disturbance than married athletes. The similarity of these patterns is probably due to younger athletes' being less educated and unmarried because they have not reached the age at which most people attend college or marry.

Athletic Background and Mood States Athletic background is another potential source of differences in mood levels among athletes. We found no mood differences when we compared athletes who had competed in high school or college to those who had competed at neither of these levels, nor when we compared athletes who worked with a coach to those who did not. Weekly training time was also unrelated to mood. However, field athletes reported greater anger than track or marathon competitors, whereas track and marathon athletes reported higher levels of vigor. Track athletes reported less fatigue than field or marathon athletes, whereas marathoners reported more fatigue than the other two groups. The fatigue factor is often confirmed when we speak to athletes who are training 70–120 miles weekly in preparation for a marathon.

Athletes who reported making highly stressful sacrifices to train for the trials also reported relatively high levels of anxiety, depression, anger, fatigue, and confusion, and low levels of vigor. These athletes also displayed relatively high levels of overall mood disturbance. In contrast, those who were highly committed to performing successfully in the trials reported less depression, fatigue, confusion, and overall mood disturbance, and greater vigor, than their less-committed counterparts. Because more-committed athletes also tended to report making more stressful sacrifices in their training process, these two influences could work in opposite directions and cancel each other out within an individual athlete.

Moods of Olympians and Non-Olympians   Ramona Pagel, the outstanding Olympic field athlete in both the shot and discus, commented on some mood swings that led to some unpredictable performance behaviors:

> "I didn't get much sleep after the Houston meet. And it was an early flight up to Ohio the next day to compete. So I had gotten on the plane, and I just fell asleep. It's like a two-hour flight up to Ohio, so I passed up breakfast on the plane. And then they drove us to the field . . . it was this huge stadium—real intimidating. For some reason I was in a good mood even though I arrived there not much before I competed. Everything seemed positive to me, even though I had the worst day of my life the previous day. My competitor threw a PR on her first throw, and then I beat her on my first throw. My second throw was an American record. If I could bottle that mood I would definitely make a lot of money!"

We examined a series of these mood swings among a larger sample of athletes. Using data from the group of athletes who completed questionnaires both before and after the Olympics, we compared mood states before the trials in the forty-four athletes who were and the 321 athletes who were not selected for the Olympic team. Olympians were significantly less depressed than non-Olympians before the trials. Olympians also showed less overall mood disturbance than non-Olympians. When only male athletes were considered, the twenty-six who made the team reported greater vigor than the 140 who did not. This finding is especially important when we consider the major indicators of overtraining and stale performance. Those athletes who were low on depression and high in vigor were most likely better prepared psychologically for the intensity of the U.S. trials.

After the Olympics, Olympians reported less anxiety than non-Olympians. This difference was particularly pronounced among track athletes. Interestingly enough, there was no statistically significant difference between team members and non-members in anxiety going into the Olympic trials. This result suggests that all elite competitors prepare for their trials with intensity, but Olympic athletes may recover faster from the trauma of a very rigorous competitive experience.

71

Changes In Mood States: Before the Trials to After the Olympics Olympian Vicki Huber again noted some insights about mood and how one best deals with daily routines:

> "I think it's too easy to feel sorry for yourself on a day where you don't feel great, and you give yourself an easier workout or you decide to give up. On some days when you feel terrific it is also easy to over-train. You feel really good, so you keep doing work on top of work, because you feel so good, you don't want to waste that feeling."

We next examined these high and low periods among our athletes during two critical periods of training.

There were small, but statistically reliable, decreases in both anxiety and fatigue in the period between April 1988 (before the trials) and October 1988 (after the Olympics). The decrease in anxiety was expected in light of the tremendous stress and pressure individuals faced when competing for a spot on the U.S. Olympic team. Athletes were no longer facing this anxiety-evoking event when they completed the October questionnaire. The decrease in anxiety was essentially limited to track athletes; it was smaller and statistically unreliable among marathoners, and both mood shifts were much smaller for field athletes. Both qualifiers and nonqualifiers experienced these mood changes, although the decrease in fatigue was much smaller (and not statistically reliable) among Olympians.

THE MEANING OF STALENESS AND BURNOUT

Jeff Atkinson, the 1,500 meter Olympic specialist, told us:

> "Runners are pretty self-obsessed people and if you don't have a coach, you don't have any balance, in my opinion. It's too easy to work too hard, work too little, blame yourself, blame other things. A coach is your voice of reason, your center point here, your fulcrum, whatever you want to call it."

What conclusions should be drawn from these comments and our research findings? How concerned should coaches, trainers, practitioners, and athletes themselves be with data from mood studies? As mentioned earlier, a coach must know something about his or her athletes and their level of intensity throughout a season or during a long training period. Without the proper diagnostic tools and sensitivity to an athlete's rhythm, too much training can diminish the quality of the ultimate return. Training too hard for too long can provide the groundwork for depression, lack of energy, staleness, and eventual burnout. Not having enough rest or diversion from an intensive training regimen can lead to a flat or stale performance. As Olympian Earl Bell commented:

> "Athletes must understand that there's only so much work you can put in, there's only so many hours in a day, there's only so much gas in the gas tank. And the trick is the quality of the work you do, not the quantity. I mean, everybody's limited on the quantity—you've only got so much energy. So the trick is to keep the quality at a high level. And to do that, you've got to train efficiently."

Most of us have heard athletes report that their training has been strong, but they had a flat race on the big day. This is a common occurrence among elite competitors and can be disastrous if the flatness falls during the Olympic trials after several intense years of preparation. Most of us hear the horror stories of the great competitor who ran great times all year, but on the big day performance had already peaked a month earlier and there was nothing left for the race of his/her life.

PREVENTION STRATEGIES

Prevention strategies for depression, athletic staleness, and burnout are numerous and call into play some creativity. Sensing that an athlete is approaching a flatness in his/her training, the coach might suggest some time off—not necessarily time out, but time off from the vigors of a typical training routine. Coaches must encourage athletes to play golf, swim, go skiing, or experience another form of exercise that is pleasurable and provides a creative diversion from the rigors of training. Olympian PattiSue Plumer put it into perspective when commenting on fatigue and staleness:

"An athlete can train herself 90 percent of the time. But everyone freaks out when they get close to major races. First of all, you can't see yourself run. So a lot of times a coach who knows you well can see things before you do. They can tell you that your legs are falling flat on the ground, your steps are heavy, or your stride is a little bit shorter. You're not leaning forward as you used to. Those are all signs of fatigue. And a good coach can pick up the cues usually faster than you can . . . that's when it's time for the pool, volleyball, biking, or a variety of cross training programs."

It has been reported that great NBA stars never stop playing during the off-season; they just modify their schedule and add a lot of creative diversity. Michael Jordan spends hours on the golf course, not to perfect his slam dunk, but to relax, keep mentally sharp, and enjoy a diversion from basketball practice. Several world-class runners use the pool as a cross training routine. In some cases, injuries force them into alternative workouts, but often they find that running in a shallow pool or swimming laps is a great way to stay well-conditioned and not burn out on twelve miles of running a day.

Another recommendation to counter low energy, depressed mood, and staleness is to encourage athletes to practice mental preparation, visualization, and relaxation skills (Porter, 1985; Ungerleider et al. 1989). The research (discussed in chapter 2) suggests that not only is this a positive diversion from training, but in fact, often enhances the quality of performance. Mental and physical relaxation periods on a daily basis allow athletes to reflect on their goals, strategies for improvement, and ways to assess progress in their training. Often, athletes become so regimented in their practice and training that they seem to have a sense of hopelessness or "where is my training leading me" attitude. Prevention strategies such as relaxation periods, listening to music during a warm-up, and time away from the target sport can add a lot to the long-term quality of athletic performance.

SUMMARY—IMPLICATIONS AND APPLICATIONS

Our data from the Elite Athlete Project suggest that entering the 1988 U.S. Olympic trials our athletes had several indicators of distress, were tired, perhaps overtrained and even depressed. As noted in the literature, overtraining can be useful and healthy when closely monitored by a coach or trainer and followed by gradual tapering of intense workouts. This allows the athlete to recover both physically and emotionally. If competitors are beginning to display symptoms of mood disturbance based on the POMS index, or any other reliable instrument, it is important to shift attention away from training schedules, modify demands on personal life, and enhance coping strategies.

As we noted earlier, our Olympic team members displayed less depression, less overall "total mood disturbance" and (among men) more energy or vigor than nonteam members. These data provide empirical evidence for the intuitive notion that positive mood and high energy may enhance the performance of even the most rigorously trained athletes. Because Olympians and non-Olympians displayed similar levels of anxiety before the trials, the data also suggest that anxiety may not necessarily impair athletic performance.

These data may also suggest that it might be useful to pay closer attention to mood and its relationship to individual competitors and their training patterns over longer periods of time. By monitoring mood and performance indicators, coaches and team consultants will avoid overtraining, staleness, and burnout which could ultimately lead to losing a very fine athletic competitor. It may be that individual athletes have different styles of coping with depression, anger, frustration, and lack of energy. Consultants and coaches need to learn more about the unique qualifications of their athletes so that mood and energy levels can be mediated and balanced against the heavy demands of training and commitment to personal lifestyles. Monitoring both physical and psychological cues are important components in the training of an elite track and field competitor. Each competitor has his/her own resources for dealing with mood swings that affect motivation and ultimately performance. As 1984 and 1988 shot and discus Olympian Ramona Pagel told us:

> "I think one of the big things that keeps me going . . . keeps me from getting stale and burned out is remembering my big throws and knowing that great feeling. I usually say to myself, Wow, I could have thrown further . . . much further. So that thought and feeling keeps me going . . . I know I can do better."

Agnew, R., & Levin, M. L. (1987). The effect of running on mood and perceived health. *Journal of Sport Behavior, 10,* 14–27.

Dishman, R. K. (1985). Medical psychology in exercise and sport. *Medical Clinics of North America, 69,* 123–43.

Farmer, M. E., Locke, B. Z., Moscicki, E. K., Dannenberg, A. L., Larson, D. B., & Radloff, L. S. (1988). Physical activity and depressive symptoms: The NHANES I epidemiologic follow-up study. *American Journal of Epidemiology, 128,* 1340–51.

Folkins, C. H., & Sime, W. E. (1981). Physical fitness training and mental health. *American Psychologist, 36,* 373–89.

Gondola, J. C., & Tuckman, B. W. (1982). Psychological mood state in "average" marathon runners. *Perceptual and Motor Skills, 55,* 1295–1300.

Gutman, M. C., Pollock M. L., Foster, C., & Schmidt, D. (1984). Training stress in Olympic speed skaters: A psychological perspective. *The Physician and Sportsmedicine, 12,* (12), 45–57.

Hagberg, J. M., Mullin, J. P., Bahrke, M., & Limburg, J. (1979). Physiological profiles and selected psychological characteristics of national class American cyclists. *Journal of Sports Medicine, 19,* 341–46.

Hughes, J. R. (1984). Psychological effects of habitual aerobic exercise: A critical review. *Preventive Medicine, 13,* 66–78.

Joesting, J. (1981). Comparison of personalities of athletes who sail with those who run. *Perceptual and Motor Skills, 52,* 514.

LeUnes, A., Hayward, S. A., & Daiss (1989). Annotated bibliography on the profile of mood states in sport, 1975–1988. *Journal of Sport Behavior, 11,* (3), 213–40.

LeUnes, A., & Nation, J. R. (1982). Saturday's heroes: A psychological portrait of college football players. *Journal of Sport Behavior, 5,* 139–49.

Lichtman, S., & Poser, E. (1983). The effects of exercise on mood and cognitive functioning. *Journal of Psychosomatic Research, 27,* 43–52.

Markoff, R., Ryan, P., & Young, T. (1982). Endorphins and mood change in long distance running. *Medicine and Science in Sports and Exercise, 14,* 11–15.

May, J. R., Veach, T. T., Reed, M. W., & Griffey, M. S. (1985). A psychological study of health, injury, and performance in athletes on the U.S. Alpine Ski Team. *Physician and Sportsmedicine, 13,* (10), 111–15.

McNair, D., Lorr, M., & Droppleman, L. (1971). *Manual for the Profile of Mood States.* San Diego: Educational and Industrial Testing Service.

Morgan, W. P. (1978, April). The mind of the marathoner. *Psychology Today,* pp. 39–40.

Morgan, W. P. (1980, July). Test of champions: The iceberg profile. *Psychology Today,* pp. 93–108.

Morgan, W. P., Brown, D. R., Raglin, J. S., O'Connor, P. J., & Ellickson, K. A. (1987). Psychological monitoring of overtraining and staleness. *British Journal of Sportsmedicine, 21,* (3), 107–14.

Morgan, W. P., & Johnson, R. (1978). Personality characteristics of successful oarsmen. *International Journal of Sport Psychology, 9,* 119–33.

Morgan, W. P., & Pollock, M. L. (1977). Psychologic characteristics of the elite distance runner. *Annals of the New York Academy of Sciences, 301,* 382–403.

Nagle, F., Morgan, W. P., Hellickson, R., Serfass, R., & Alexander, J. (1975). Spotting success in trials in Olympic contenders. *Physician and Sportsmedicine, 3,* (12), 31–34, 84.

Porter, K. (1985). Psychological characteristics of the average female runner. *Physician and Sportsmedicine, 13,* (5), 171–75.

Ross, C. E., & Hayes, D. (1988). Exercise and psychologic well-being in the community. *American Journal of Epidemiology, 127,* 762–71.

Silva, J. M., III, Shultz, B. B., Haslam, R. W., Martin, T. P., & Murray, D. F. (1985). Discriminating characteristics of contestants at the United States Olympic wrestling trials. *International Journal of Sport Psychology, 16,* 79–102.

Taylor, C. B., Sallis, J. F., & Needle, R. (1985). The relation of physical activity and exercise to mental health. *Public Health Reports, 100,* 195–202.

Ungerleider, S., & Golding, J. (1989) Mood profiles of Masters track and field athletes. *Perceptual and Motor Skills, 68,* 607–17.

Ungerleider, S., Golding, J., Porter, K., & Foster, J. (1989, July). Mental advantages for Masters: A psychological study of 1,014 Masters athletes finds that some things do improve with age. *Running Times 150,* pp. 18–20.

CHAPTER 5

"It's always something! Either you get hurt or you get a cold because you're under a lot of stress and you're really tense, and you know you have to make the team. Performance is what keeps you under contract with shoe companies, what gets you your rankings from TAC, the Olympic Committee, your monthly income. You've got to be on top a lot of times, and I think it's really stressful for somebody at my level. I think a lot of things pop up at the wrong time!"

Brian Abshire
1988 U.S. Olympic Team
3,000 Meter Steeplechase

Stress, Injury, and Illness

O ver the past twenty-five years a large body of evidence has accumulated suggesting a direct relationship between stressful life events and the onset of physical and psychological illness (Rahe & Arthur, 1978). Changes in life-style patterns have been linked to everything from heart disease (Rahe, Bennett & Romo, 1973) to schizophrenia (Brown & Birley, 1968) to traffic accidents (Selzer & Vinokur, 1974). Therefore, it is not surprising that life events are now being found to have a significant influence on the health and performance of the elite athlete (Anderson & Williams, 1988; May & Sieb, 1987). If death of a family member, divorce, moving to a new city, or changes in sleeping patterns can increase one's chances of contracting a disease or crashing a car, it seems as though these life changes might have dramatic impact on one's athletic pursuits, including the potential for sustaining an injury.

STRESSFUL LIFE EVENTS AND INJURY RISK

Several studies provide evidence that stressful life events are related to decrements in athletic health and performance. In 1975, Bramwell and colleagues developed the Social and Athletic Readjustment Rating Scale (SARRS) in order to examine the role life stresses play in the onset of athletic injuries. The SARRS is an adaptation for athletes of the widely used Social Readjustment Rating Scale (SRRS) constructed by Holmes and Rahe (1967) as a measure of social events and life situations. In administering the SARRS to seventy-nine University of Washington varsity football players, Bramwell and his colleagues found that these players, with a few minor exceptions, did not differ in their assessment of the significance of life events from an average middle-class American population. A high correlation was obtained between the rankings of life events in the SARRS football sample and the SRRS life events rankings by the Holmes and Rahe general American sample, suggesting that the attitudes and values of these athletes reflect those of the larger society.

A second discovery was that players suffering major time-loss injuries (those missing three or more practices and/or one or more games because of specific injury) had significantly higher SARRS scores prior to injury than noninjured players. The injury rate for players with low SARRS scores (0 to 399) was 30%, with medium scores (400 to 799) was 50%, and high scores (800 plus) was 73%. From these data the authors concluded that the risk of an injury to a football player increases in direct relationship to the accumulation of challenging and stressful life events.

In a similar study, Coddington and Troxell (1980) modified the fifty-seven-item SARRS into a fifty-item Life Events Scale for Adolescents (LES-A) This instrument was used as a measure of family events, including situations in which adolescents have no control, and in some cases experience major family dysfunction. When the LES-A was administered to 114 high school football players, Coddington and Troxell found that players experiencing family instability were more likely to sustain an injury. The risk of an injury for a boy losing a parent was *five times greater* than for a boy experiencing no family losses.

A third look into the relationship between life change and athletic injury, also involving football players, comes from the work of Passer and Seese (1983). Their major focus was whether life stress should be conceptualized in terms of total life change (Dohrenwend, 1973) or only undesirable change (Mueller, Edwards & Yarvis, 1977). Passer and Seese compared the degree to which desirable vs. undesirable life change was related to injury. They examined the role of general trait anxiety, competitive trait anxiety, and locus of control. Using 104 varsity football players from two different sized universities, the researchers found that players from the smaller (Division II) school showed a positive relationship between high levels of negative life change events and athletic injury. However, positive life events were unrelated to injury.

Each of these three studies suggests, in part, that a change in life events places an athlete at a higher risk of becoming injured. The life stress/athletic injury model is based primarily on the assumption that the two chief mechanisms responsible for the relationship are increases in muscle tension and deficits in attention during stress (Anderson & Williams, 1988). If one accepts this assumption, then the findings concerning such a high physical contact sport as football should not be terribly surprising. However, most sports, including track and field, do not involve the extreme level of contact that football does, nor do they place the athlete at such a high immediate risk of sustaining an injury. Therefore, data involving other less physically strenuous sports may be of greater relevance to the majority of elite athletes.

May and colleagues (1985a) administered the SARRS to ninety-seven elite male and female athletes representing five sports (biathlon, race walking, figure skating, gymnastics, and basketball) at the U.S. Olympic Training Center in Colorado Springs. One year later, each athlete completed a Health, Injury, and Performance Survey (HIPS) measuring frequency, duration, and severity of any injuries or illnesses suffered in the last year. Questions on individual performance were also included. Findings indicated that scores on the SARRS differed significantly by type of sport. Of the five sports studied, basketball players had the highest life change scores followed by gymnasts, race walkers, biathletes, and figure skaters. The researchers contended that these differences were probably a function of age rather than sport per se, with younger athletes being more vulnerable to the effects of life stresses.

Significant relationships were also found between the SARRS and HIPS, with correlations existing between life change scores and frequency of headaches, musculoskeletal leg and feet problems, anxiety, weight changes, and abuse of nonprescribed substances. Unfortunately, no information on specific substances was reported in this research. Many of these health problems were related to type of sport. For example, figure skaters reported relatively high degrees of neurological problems and sleep loss, whereas gymnasts indicated a greater concern with increased use of coffee and tea, as well as digestive and weight problems. These results are consistent with the serious concerns about anorexia nervosa and bulimia among gymnasts.

May and colleagues (1985a) attempted to identify health and injury problems associated with specific life changes, but no significant findings were obtained. In terms of performance, the researchers found that national rankings were not significantly related to life change scores, yet regional rankings did show a strong correlation with life change scores. In a related study, May et al. (1985b) had seventy-three members of the U.S. Alpine Ski Team fill out the SARRS, LES-A, measures of well-being and depressive symptoms, and the HIPS. Athletes who scored high on one stress measure tended to score high on the other one.

Those scoring high on either stress scale reported more depressive symptoms and lower levels of well-being. Furthermore, life events, less well-being, and depression were all significantly related to the frequency and duration of many health problems suffered by skiers. These include ear, nose, and throat problems, headaches, anxiety, digestive disorders, sleep disturbances, and the abuse of nonprescription substances such as tobacco and drugs.

LITERATURE SUMMARY

Previous research indicates that stressful life events are associated with athletic injuries. Although the most consistent evidence comes from research on contact sports (specifically football), a few studies of noncontact sports report similar findings. Research also suggests that stress among athletes is associated with illness. These results raise several interesting questions. Which athletes are at greatest risk for stress? What are the consequences of stress, other than injury? Are highly-stressed athletes who do not sustain an injury at greater risk of impaired performance? Does the athlete's method of coping with injury affect this risk? Can we predict which athletes are likely to use various coping methods? We used data from the Elite Athlete Project to examine these issues.

RESULTS FROM THE ELITE ATHLETE PROJECT

We measured stress in the 1988 Olympic trials contenders using the Social and Athletic Readjustment Rating Scale (SARRS) (Bramwell, Masuda, Wagner & Holmes, 1975). This questionnaire was originally constructed by adding to the Social Readjustment Rating Scale (SRRS) items relating to athletic participation and deleting items not relevant to a male college football sample. Therefore, we decided to examine overall stress scores using the complete fifty-six-item scale, and to break this scale down into two subscales: a life events scale consisting of forty-one items—those events not related to athleticism; and a subscale with fifteen items relating solely to athletic endeavors.

We reasoned that the effect of nonathletic events or life occurrences might be so pervasive that it could have a powerful influence on a person's athletic career. On the other hand, athletic stress may be significant because of its direct relation to training and competition. Earl Bell, the four-time Olympic pole vaulter, shed some light on the importance of one kind of athletic stress:

> "I have trouble with my back, so I see a specialist and he gets the tension out and gets the body back in balance. Before you know it, my mind—which is a very important component in all of this—comes back in focus, and my attitude's back where it should be. The number one mistake athletes make is overtraining and that is very stressful. It's far and away the number one problem that people have to realize."

Which Athletes Are at Greatest Risk for Stress?

We looked further at the issue of who is at risk for stressful life events as a function of demographic characteristics. Younger elite athletes reported more stress in both the athletic and life events scale on both of our survey questionnaires. This finding is consistent with general population research, which indicates that younger people report more stressful life events than older people (Golding, Potts, & Aneshensel, 1991). Less-educated athletes, who tended to be younger, reported more stress on the life events scale between April and October. Similarly, unmarried athletes, who also tended to be younger, reported more athletic and life events stress on both questionnaires than did married athletes. We found no gender difference in either subscale, consistent with nonathlete populations (Dean & Ensel, 1983; Goldberg & Comstock, 1980; Golding et al. 1991; Masuda & Holmes, 1978).

We next examined whether stress was more common in athletes specializing in specific sports. When looking at stress among track, field, and marathon athletes, controlling statistically for age, we found that field athletes appear to experience more stress than the other two groups. The relationship of other athletic characteristics to stressful life events was also of interest to us. Athletes who have a coach reported more athletic stress than those who don't. This result suggests that having a coach provides the opportunity for an athlete to be challenged more, pushed harder in workouts, and even to experience stress.

Another possibility is that some kinds of athletic stress are only possible for athletes with a coach. For example, athletes who do not have a coach will not report the event "trouble with head coach." Because most teams are coached, athletes who do not have a coach are unlikely to be on a team, and thus will not report events such as "being dropped from team."

On the April questionnaire, athletes who trained for longer hours reported more stress, particularly athletic stress. Again, it is possible that this relationship represents the opportunity to experience stress: the more hours an athlete spends training, the more that athlete is in a situation in which athletic stress can occur. Alternatively, these athletes may have been training extra hours to cope with stressful situations associated with their athletic participation. An athlete who had trouble with the coach (an athletic stress) might train for extra hours to improve skills and thus avoid conflict with the coach. Finally, athletes who competed in high school or college reported greater stress on both questionnaires.

Consequences of Stress When we compared Olympians with non-Olympians, those who qualified for the team reported significantly less overall stress ($M = 230.9$) in the year before the U.S. trials than those who did not ($M = 281.4$). This result is consistent with previous research (Anderson & Williams, 1988; May & Sieb, 1987) on athletes in contact (Bramwell, et al. 1975; Coddington & Troxell, 1980; Passer & Seese, 1983) and noncontact sports (May, et al. 1985a, 1985b). This pattern was similar when only the life events scale was considered, with Olympians' average score (184.7) significantly lower than that of athletes who did not make the team ($M = 224.1$). There was no significant difference between the two groups in the athletic stress index. In addition, *after* the trials, there was no difference in stress levels between Olympian and non-Olympian elite athletes. This suggests that certain athletes, although physiologically similar, do differ on how they perceive and respond to stressful situations. Olympic gold medalist in the 4 × 400 relay, Danny Everett, has noted:

"I suffer from asthma . . . so I constantly worry about having a flare-up on the track. But I also know that if I have a reaction, I'm well prepared because I work on these things in training and practice. I just try and breathe through it and my breathing leads to a sense of relaxation and well-being."

85

This psychosocial difference may influence a major performance such as the U.S. trials and/or the Olympic Games. It is noteworthy that, after the stress of the trials, elite athletes seemed to return to baseline levels of stress with no differences between qualifiers and nonqualifiers.

We suspected that less-stressed athletes might be more likely to make the team because their lower stress levels would allow them to be more relaxed, more focused, and therefore less likely to be injured. It seemed possible that the injury, not the stress level in and of itself, would account for whether the athlete made the team. To examine this possibility, we looked at the associations of stressful life events with injury. Not surprisingly, we found that athletes who reported higher stress in the year before the U.S. trials were also more likely to be injured during that year. Highly-stressed athletes were also more likely to have an injury lasting at least three days (i.e., it was at least three days before the athlete could train again) than less-stressed athletes. This finding has strong implications for sports consultants, coaches, and psychologists. Being aware of athletes' stress levels throughout the training process could mean being able to offer some guidance for how and when to taper, as well as when an athlete might peak in the training cycle. If stress levels are too high, vulnerability may be increased and injury potential is very real. Evaluating stress levels every few months should be an important prevention measure for coaches and consultants.

However, in spite of highly-stressed athletes' greater risk of injury, injured athletes were not less likely to be selected for the Olympic team. Although injury is important in and of itself, it did not explain why more-stressed athletes were less likely to be selected for the team.

Another possibility is that low stress levels played an indirect role in team selection by improving mood. Olympians were less depressed, and showed less overall mood disturbance, than non-Olympians (see chapter 4). All POMS mood scales, including depression and overall mood disturbance, were higher in highly-stressed athletes, whether athletic or life events stress was considered, both before and after the trials. This suggests the possibility that stressed athletes became depressed, and, perhaps by interfering with their focus or fine tuning, their depression and overall mood disturbance may have hindered their performance in the U.S. trials.

Athletic Injuries

Recommendations to monitor athletes' stress levels to help prevent injury take on additional importance for elite athletes when we consider that athletic injury is very common in this population. Almost all the elite athletes in our study (92%) have experienced injury at some time in their life, and nearly half reported being injured one to three months prior to the 1988 Olympic trials. This is significant and deserves additional attention in regard to training and overtraining practices. In the year before the trials, the most prevalent injury was a strained muscle or tendon problem experienced by about two-thirds of the athletes who had injuries lasting three days or more. Other athletes reported a torn tendon or muscle (e.g., Achilles rupture) (11%), strained back (8%), torn ligament (7%), broken bone (6%), and, occasionally, a dislocated joint (2%). A similar rank order was observed when injuries between the time of the trials and the Olympic Games was considered. Of the injured athletes, about a third could train again after ten days or less of recovery, and one-fifth could train again after only five days of rest and rehabilitation. The average amount of time all injured athletes took for recovery was thirty-six days. This is a significant amount of time loss considering the vast number of hours our athletes spend in daily workouts.

Three thousand-meter Olympic champion PattiSue Plumer gave us some insight into the experience of dealing with injury:

"I was in a cast for a month, and then I couldn't walk for a month. When I started to jog again I had a series of recurring injuries in the same place due to the fact that my bone wasn't strong enough to sustain my running. So it took a lot of false starts. I'd jog for two or three weeks and then, the first solid workout I would do, I would be re-injured, or broken again. The actual bone itself wouldn't heal. In fact, even after the nine months was over I went and had a bone scan. And that area of the bone was still not completely healed. And that was a year later. I then had a series of stress fractures in the fibula and apparently the bone had demineralized, trying to heal the other injury. It was difficult times for me!"

Which Athletes Are at Greatest Risk for Injury? To learn more about what types of injury occur and who suffers them, we subjected our data to several analyses. Men were more likely to be injured than women according to our data on both questionnaires. There were no age, social class, or marital status differences in injury. When specific types of injury were examined, women were less likely to have a torn tendon, but there were no gender differences in other kinds of injuries. More-educated athletes were less likely to report strained tendons and more likely to report torn tendons. There were no demographic differences in type of injury between the trials and the Olympic Games.

There were no differences in risk of injury for track, field, and marathon athletes in the year before the trials. When specific injuries were explored for a twelve-month period, track athletes were more likely to report strained tendons and less likely to report a strained back or torn ligament, whereas field athletes showed the reverse pattern. In the period between the trials and the games, marathoners were less likely than track or field athletes to report an injury lasting at least three days. Among athletes injured during this period, there were no differences in specific injury by type of sport.

During the year before the trials, athletes with high school or college competition experience were more likely to report an injury, and more likely to report an injury lasting at least three days, than those without such experience. Having prior experience as a collegiate athlete does not offer the advantage of greater wisdom, but suggests that some athletes might be wearing down a bit earlier in their career.

Stress and Injury Olympian PattiSue Plumer gave us some insight about injury and alternative strategies for dealing with injury:

> "I've had this long-term injury, which was a plantar fascitis problem. What worked for me as far as healing was concerned was acupuncture, and part of my therapist's treatment of that injury, especially at the beginning, was leaving the needles in my foot and my leg for about

forty-five minutes. And the reason why he would do that is because he wanted me to stay relaxed, but also to visualize some of the hot spots. And I would often visualize, with my eyes closed, and in my mind I would see a bright red spot—which would be the injury. And I would try to turn this spot into a dim light if I could, making it black, making the bright red spot or injury turn to a healing color of black."

We wanted to learn more about visualization, stress, and injury as well as the recovery process.

We noted earlier that athletes with high stress levels in the year before the trials also reported high rates of injury during that period. Athletes with high stress levels during the period between the trials and the games were at high risk for injury during that period as well. In addition, athletes who reported high athletic stress levels in the year before the trials were at increased risk for injuries lasting three days or longer during the six-month period following the trials. One possible explanation for this finding is that athletes who had high stress levels in the year before the trials, and therefore were more likely to report injury before the trials, were more vulnerable to injury soon after the trials because of their earlier injuries. This finding has significant ramifications for understanding the health and well-being of athletes who make the team and progress to the Olympic Games. Stress and injury may play an important role in athletic outcome.

Mood and Injury Athletes who had been injured at some time in their lives were more anxious than those who had never been injured. Those who had been injured for at least three days at some time during the year before the trials reported greater anxiety than noninjured athletes. Athletes who had been injured during that previous year also reported greater anger in some analyses. This pattern suggests that injured athletes are at risk for anxiety, and possibly anger. On the other hand, athletes who were relatively anxious or angry at the time of the April questionnaire were more likely than their calmer counterparts to be injured for at least three days during the six months following the trials. Anxiety, anger, fatigue, confusion, and overall mood disturbance during that six-month period were also related to a greater probability of significant injury. Thus, anxious, angry athletes appeared to be at greater risk of injury.

Taken together, these results suggest a two-way relationship between anxiety and anger on the one hand, and injury on the other. We can speculate that athletes may respond to injury with anxiety about future competition, further injury, or a sense of general vulnerability, and with anger about being hurt and being unable to train. We can also speculate that these emotions may increase the athlete's risk for further injury. The combination of anxiety and anger resembles the Type A personality construct, which may be related to heart disease (O'Rourke, Houston, Harris & Snyder, 1988), suggesting a possible link between Type A behavior and athletic injury. This angry and anxious phenomenon could lead to a cycle of diminished performance and diminished returns for the athlete. Learning about an athlete's response to injury could give us clues to more healthy intervention strategies.

Injury and Team Selection Margaret Groos, the Olympic marathoner, spoke candidly about a serious illness:

> "I had a hypothyroid disease they recently diagnosed and it was physically just debilitating. I didn't know what was wrong with me, and it was really horrible. I had everyone telling me it was in my head and that I really secretly didn't want to run, and I was trying to sabotage myself, and . . . it was really hard. I could not run more than ten minutes before I would have to stop with complete fatigue. I could not run or do anything active. So once I was recovered, and on the comeback, the hardest thing was trusting my body. Because I was so conditioned to going out and trying as hard as I could mentally and being ready mentally, but not having the body. And it took a good two years of training and racing before I got my racing head back. It just took a lot of mental practice remembering, trying to remember what it was like to go through a race and have your body in tune with your mind. And I think that really hurts younger athletes when they first get injured, if you kind of lose that sync with your mind and body, you have to remember what it was like when you were healthy."

We took a closer look at long-term injury and illness to see how they affected team selection.

Surprisingly, injured athletes were no less likely to be selected for the Olympic team than were noninjured athletes. Neither were there differences between team members and non-team members when specific types of injury were considered. It is possible that Olympians sustained fewer injuries, or were injured earlier in the year before the trials, than non-Olympians. It is also possible that injured athletes chose a path of denial and did not personally disclose their injuries for fear of being eliminated from the U.S. team. There is some anecdotal evidence from sports medicine personnel that some athletes who had serious injuries continued to train after team selection because they didn't want to relinquish their precious slot on the team. These athletes knew that once in Korea they would not be able to compete fully in the Olympic Games but did not want to give up a slight glimmer of hope.

Our research team was also curious about the way athletes coped with injury and how coping strategies affected their chances of team selection. Therefore, we next examined the athletes' coping strategies when injured.

Coping with Injuries

Don and Debbi Lawrence are husband and wife, and members of the U.S. Race Walk Team. Don Lawrence noted:

> "In dealing with injuries, we gain strength through positive workouts. We never let pain creep in our minds. You know, we accept that negatives are out there, but we're going to keep them out there. We try to draw energy from each other, which is kind of a unique situation, because Debbi and I are together twenty-four hours a day. In fact, we've gone to the point that when one is injured—instead of one of us going out and race walking and the other staying at home or riding the bike that day, we've arranged to have treadmills downstairs so that we can continue to work together and support each other . . . even through injury."

To understand coping responses to injury, we asked the athletes how well they coped with their injuries and what methods they used. They ranked both physical and mental coping from "not at all well" to "extremely well." The most common response to both questions was "moderately well," chosen by one-fifth of our athletes regarding physical coping and one-fifth regarding mental coping. We also asked athletes about the methods they used to cope with injury. We chose categories of coping methods on the basis of open-ended responses to similar questions in two previous studies of over 1,000 Masters track and field athletes. To cope physically with injuries occurring in the year before the trials, six out of ten athletes used alternative training strategies, such as swimming; two-thirds sought help from a physician, physical therapist, or other health professional; one-third rested completely; and four out of ten continued training at a decreased level of intensity. To cope mentally, one-fourth of the athletes relaxed; fewer than a fifth used imagery to heal the injury; three-fourths of our sample accepted being injured and used patience; about a third became depressed; and nearly half became frustrated. Similar patterns were seen for coping with injuries occurring between April and October. We can speculate that a combination of coping strategies may be most effective. For example, Brian Abshire, the 3,000 meter steeplechase Olympian, commented in this regard:

> "Probably the most important thing in coping with injury was getting proper medical attention, then seeing a sports consultant, and learning some relaxation strategies. I needed to put the injury out of my mental picture. All of those things helped me get beyond the injury."

Mac Wilkins, the four-time Olympian, told us he found imagery effective as a coping strategy and in helping to heal an injury:

> "I think in 1979 I had some low-grade chronic knee soreness. I did a lot of visualization about cleaning the area out and getting rid of the pain and making things heal up and getting back in order. And that seemed to help. In fact, it almost seemed to be a temporary pain reliever."

Evaluation of physical coping was unrelated to the athlete's actual choice of physical coping responses, possibly because the best physical response to a specific injury depends on the nature and severity of the injury. Indeed, we found that both before and after the trials, athletes tended *not* to cope with longer-lasting injuries by continuing their usual activity with decreased intensity. After the trials, athletes with longer-lasting injuries were more likely to report resting completely, and were less satisfied with their physical coping strategies.

In contrast, athletes who relaxed and who accepted being injured evaluated their mental coping more favorably, whereas those who became depressed or frustrated were relatively unfavorable in their evaluations. During the period between the trials and the games, athletes with longer-lasting injuries were less satisfied with their mental coping strategies, and, understandably, more likely to be depressed.

Athletic Characteristics Related to Coping Responses
Track athletes tended to assess their physical and mental coping efforts relatively favorably, and marathoners relatively unfavorably, on the April questionnaire. In October, field athletes were most favorable, and marathoners least favorable, in their impressions of their mental coping. Carmen Troncoso, the second place finisher in the U.S. Olympic trials in the 5,000 meters noted:

> "I have had some nasty injuries, but I usually know when I am able to race. Once race day comes, I can usually block out mentally any physical pain or discomfort and focus on the race."

When physical coping in the year before the trials was examined, track athletes were relatively unlikely to use alternate activities or see a medical professional, whereas marathoners were more likely to use alternative activities or rest. With regard to coping mentally, track athletes reported high levels of acceptance and low levels of depression and frustration, whereas marathoners showed the reverse pattern. In addition, marathoners were less likely to report relaxing.

Athletes training with a coach assessed their physical coping strategies in the year before the trials more favorably than did those without a coach, and were also less likely to report frustration. This suggests that the influence of a coach is not only for enhancement of training technique, but for a more comprehensive support system that assists in dealing with injury and coping with the frustration of not being able to train.

In training for the race of her life after coming off injuries and a short recuperation period, PattiSue Plumer noted:

"I was out of shape and I'd been real sick and hadn't been able to start training at all that year until March and the Olympic Trials were in July. So that meant that we really could only go with one race strategy. And it was either going to work, or it wasn't. We didn't have time to plan for everything, and we didn't have the conditioning to plan for everything, and so we bet, we gambled basically. We gambled on one race strategy, and that was either going to work or it wasn't. Luckily it worked. But because of that one strategy plan, it was very easy for me . . . I knew exactly what I had to do."

Athletes who trained for longer hours before the trials were more likely to report using alternate activities and seeking medical help for injuries, and less likely to report complete rest (on both questionnaires), than athletes who trained less. This makes sense because medical consultation and alternate strategies allow continuation of activity, which contributes to longer training hours, whereas rest decreases training hours by definition. However, these athletes described their mental coping strategies less favorably, and reported greater depression and frustration, than athletes who trained less. On the other hand, athletes who trained for longer hours were more likely to report using imagery to heal their injuries.

Athletes with high school or college competition experience tended to rate their physical and mental coping strategies in the year before the trials favorably, possibly because of their long experience in using such strategies. They also were more likely than others to report complete rest and less likely to report frustration on both of our survey questionnaires.

Consequences of Coping Responses We wondered whether some methods of coping with injury were related to an increased chance of being selected for the Olympic team. Physical coping responses were unrelated to team selection, and Olympians did not cope differently from non-Olympians after the trials. The only coping strategy distinguishing qualifiers from nonqualifiers was *imagery*. Athletes who used imagery to heal injuries sustained during the year before the trials were more likely to qualify for the Olympic team than those who did not use imagery. This finding raises the possibility that it is not being injured that affects team selection, but how one deals with the injury; specifically, whether one uses imagery to cope with it. Athletes with higher athletic and life event stress levels in the year before the trials were also more likely to use imagery to cope with injury, suggesting that these athletes responded productively to stress, with favorable results for their performance. It is possible that athletes used imagery to engage in mental practice when they could not practice physically, and thereby maintained or improved their skills to a greater extent than injured athletes who did not use imagery. Another possibility is that athletes used imagery to visualize the injury healing, and that this technique was effective, allowing better performance in the trials than would otherwise have been possible.

SUMMARY—IMPLICATIONS AND APPLICATIONS

Athletes who qualified for the Olympic team reported significantly less life event stress in the year before the trials than those who did not. Athletes who reported higher stress during that year were also more likely to be injured. However, injured athletes were no less likely to be selected for the Olympic team than were noninjured athletes. It is possible that low stress levels played an indirect role in team selection, because less-stressed athletes were also less depressed, and less-depressed athletes were more likely to qualify for the team. Another possibility is that it was not injury in and of itself, but the athlete's response to injury, that was related to team selection. Specifically, athletes who used imagery to heal injuries sustained during the year before the trials were more likely to qualify for the Olympic team than injured athletes who did not use imagery.

It appears that imagery and visualization are not only training strategies as discussed in chapter 2, but might, in fact, be a "life and survival" strategy for the complete athlete. Coaches and sports consultants may need to focus on a two-tiered approach to implementing mental practice techniques in the future. On the one level, strategies may encompass imagery and visualization for athletic skill enhancement, and a second tier might assist athletes with coping strategies to heal injured bodies. Strategies involved in the first tier might also be useful for the second. Olympic pole vaulter Earl Bell provided this example:

"I just took a couple of weeks off because I'd kind of gotten to a point of almost exhaustion and I needed some physical therapy to help get everything all lined up again. But the whole time I'm resting I still do workouts in my head."

These results again point to the importance of mood for athletic performance (see chapter 4), and to the potential usefulness of imagery as a training technique (see chapter 2).

Tools for measuring stressful life events such as the SARRS should not be used on an individual basis as predictors of when, where, and to whom injuries will occur. However, when used carefully, information about stressful life events may alert athletes and their advocates to factors influencing susceptibility to injury. This might assist in appropriate prevention of injury and other health risks that may impair peak performance.

References

Anderson, M. B., & Williams, J. M. (1988). A model of stress and athletic injury: Prediction and prevention. *Journal of Sport and Exercise Psychology, 10,* 294–306.

Bramwell, S. T., Masuda, M., Wagner, N. N., & Holmes, T. H. (1975). Psychological factors in athletic injuries: Development and application of the Social and Athletic Readjustment Rating Scale (SARRS). *Journal of Human Stress, 1,* 6–20.

Brown, G. W., & Birley, J. L. (1968). Crises and life changes and the onset of schizophrenia. *Journal of Health and Social Behavior, 9,* 203–14.

Coddington, R., & Troxell, J. (1980). The effects of emotional factors on football injury rates: A pilot study. *Journal of Human Stress, 4,*(6), 2–6.

Dean, A., & Ensel, W. M. (1983). Socially structured depression in men and women. *Research in Community and Mental Health, 3,* 113–39.

Dohrenwend, B. S. (1973). Life events as stressors: A methodological inquiry. *Journal of Health and Social Behavior, 14,* 167–75.

Goldberg, E. L., & Comstock, G. W. (1980). Epidemiology of life events: Frequency in general populations. *American Journal of Epidemiology, 111,* 736–52.

Golding, J. M., Potts, M. K., & Aneshensel, C. S. (1991). Stress exposure among Mexican Americans and non-Hispanic Whites. *Journal of Community Psychology, 19,* 37–59.

Holmes, T. H., & Rahe, R. H. (1967). The Social Readjustment Rating Scale. *Journal of Psychosomatic Research, 11,* 213–18.

Lloyd, C. (1980). Life events and depressive disorder reviewed: II. Events as precipitating factors. *Archives of General Psychiatry, 37,* 541–48.

Masuda, M., & Holmes, T. H. (1978). Life events: Perceptions and frequencies. *Psychosomatic Medicine, 40,* 236–61.

May, J. R., & Sieb, G. E. (1987). Athletic injuries: Psychosocial factors in the onset, sequelae, rehabilitation, and prevention. In J. R. May & M. J. Asken (Eds.), *Sport psychology* (pp. 157–85). Costa Mesa, CA: PMA Publishing.

May, J. R., Veach, T. T., Reed, M. W., & Griffey, M. S. (1985a). A psychological study of health, injury, and performance in athletes on the U.S. Alpine Ski Team. *The Physician and Sportsmedicine, 13,*(10), 111–15.

May, J. R., Veach, T. L., Southard, S. W., & Herring, M. W. (1985b). The effects of life change on injuries, illnesses, and performance in elite athletes. In N. K. Butts, T. T. Gushiken, & B. Zarins (Eds.), *The elite athlete* (pp. 171–79). New York: Spectrum Publications.

Mueller, D. P., Edwards, D. W., & Yarvis, R. M. (1977). Stressful life events and psychiatric symptomatology: Change or undesirability? *Journal of Health and Social Behavior, 18,* 307–17.

O'Rourke, D. F., Houston, B. K., Harris, J. K., & Snyder, C. R. (1988). The Type A behavior pattern: Summary, conclusions, and implications. In B. K. Houston & C. R. Snyder (Eds.), *Type A behavior pattern: Research, theory, and intervention.* New York: Wiley.

Passer, M. W., & Seese, M. D. (1983). Life stress and athletic injury: Examination of positive versus negative events and three moderator variables. *Journal of Human Stress, 9,* (4), 11–16.

Rahe, R. H., & Arthur, R. J. (1978). Life change and illness studies: Past history and future directions. *Journal of Human Stress, 4,* (1), 3–15.

Rahe, R. H., Bennett, M., & Romo, J. (1973). Subjects recent life changes and coronary heart disease in Finland. *American Journal of Psychiatry, 130,* 1222–26.

Selzer, M. L., & Vinokur, A. (1974). Life events, subjective stress, and traffic accidents. *American Journal of Psychiatry, 131,* (8), 903–6.

CHAPTER 6

"After the Olympic trials, everyone was calling—I mean people that I didn't even know were offering me money and stuff. It was great and I was getting interviewed from media and newspapers all over the country. And then after the Olympics, I didn't come home with a medal—so things changed. No one was calling me! And I thought—people are just your friends if you're a world champion . . . and this hurt a lot to see this attitude. It made me think a lot about elite athletics . . . and I had to step back a few paces and make a few decisions about my life and priorities. It was time to go back to school and get my degree."

Gary Kinder
1988 U.S. Olympic Team
Decathlon

Coping, Stress, and Social Support

STRESS AND THE ELITE ATHLETE

I n the previous chapter, we examined ways in which elite athletes cope with being injured. Another source of stress that is common to virtually all of these athletes is the stress of competition itself. In this chapter we examine the ways in which these elite athletes coped with the stress of competition, and how their perceptions of the trials and their personal, athletic, and social characteristics were related to those coping efforts.

Up until now, we have taken the meaning of *stress* for granted, implicitly equating it with events that cause change in a person's life. That is one of the most common definitions of stress. However, stress has probably been defined in as many ways as it has been experienced. We adopted the definition of Lazarus and Folkman (1984), who define stress as "demands (external or internal) that are appraised as taxing or exceeding the resources of the person." External demands include confronting a strong opponent in an important contest; whereas internal demands include goals, personal standards of behavior relating to values or commitment, or unconscious motives and conflicts.

Stress is usually seen as coming from one of three sources: life events, such as those measured by the SARRS (see chapter 5), which indicate relatively major changes in the person's life; ongoing stressful conditions or strains (Brown & Harris, 1978); and smaller, day-to-day events or daily hassles (Kanner, Coyne, Schaefer & Lazarus, 1981). All of these have been found to be related to emotional distress in nonathletes (Brown & Harris, 1978; Kanner et al. 1981; Lloyd, 1980), and all are probably applicable to an athletic context. An example of an ongoing stressful condition specific to an athlete might be lack of money to live on while training. An example of a sport-specific daily hassle might be a telephone ringing during a mental practice session. Although we can speculate that both strains and hassles may affect athletes' well-being and performance, and future research should address this issue, we focus here on one example of an important stressful event in the life of an athlete: competition in the Olympic trials.

An event is only a source of stress if the person sees it as threatening or challenging to herself or himself (Lazarus &

Folkman, 1984). For example, internal demands can be stressful if they threaten self-esteem:

> "It is one's perception of inadequacy in successfully meeting the performance demands, and their perceptions of the consequences of failure, that create the threat to self-esteem which triggers the stress reaction" (Scanlon, 1984).

What Is So Stressful about Athletics? Anyone who has played Little League baseball, pick-up basketball, or just shared a friendly set of tennis on Sunday morning, knows that competition, at any level, has the potential to spark all kinds of anxious, aggressive, and other less-than-desirable emotions in even the most calm and otherwise psychologically stable individuals. People experience various levels of anxiety prior to competitive situations, often as a result of the positive or negative consequences of competition over an individual's history (Martens, 1977). One of these consequences may be changes in self-esteem. Martens (1977) defined competitive trait anxiety as the tendency to perceive competitive situations as threatening to self-esteem. The fact that an athlete has made it to the top of her or his sport is by no means evidence that he or she is immune to the stress of competitive endeavors. The prospect of competition in and of itself may not be particularly unsettling, yet there are plenty of elements within high-level competition that take their psychological toll on even the best athletes.

Fears of failure and resulting social disapproval are the most common sources of stress in athletes (Feigley, 1985; Grimsley & Bunn, 1987; Smith, 1980). According to Smith (1980), high stress athletes' thought processes are typically dominated by fears of the catastrophic consequences of failure to live up to their own and others' expectations. Other common sources of stress specific to athletes include injury, defeat, fatigue, overtraining and staleness, media attention, problems with teammates and coaches, inactivity, and poor officiating (Bramwell, Masuda, Wagner & Holmes, 1975; Buceta, 1985; Grimsley & Bunn, 1987; May & Sieb, 1987; Murphy, 1986; Scanlon, 1984; Smith, 1986; Stafford, 1984; Weiss & Troxel, 1986).

This anxiety and fear of failure may be compounded for elite athletes. Sports are supposed to be enjoyable, and for most people this is the main reason for participating in them. At the elite level, however, enjoyment is usually superseded by commitment and hard work as sports become a job, a career, a way of life. The fact that an athlete's professional and financial livelihood often rests on a competitive outcome often leads to magnification of a highly stressful situation.

In summary, elite athletes are by no means a special breed, independent of the population as a whole. However, they do lead a unique life-style which exposes them to specific types and levels of stress foreign to many people involved in less physically and emotionally demanding endeavors. Therefore, a key challenge for those interested in the psychology of sport is to continue to integrate what is known about the stress and coping patterns of people in general into research efforts aimed at exploring these same issues in athletes across a variety of different activities.

COPING

Lazarus and Folkman (1984) define coping as "the cognitive and behavioral efforts to master, tolerate, or reduce" stress. Coping strategies can be classified in several ways. For example, Lazarus and Folkman (1984) distinguish between problem-focused and emotion-focused coping strategies. Problem-focused coping refers to behaviors intended to change the situation that the person perceives as stressful. For example, if an athlete perceives competing against a particular opponent as stressful, that athlete might choose not to enter races in which that opponent was competing. Emotion-focused coping refers to efforts to change the way one feels about a stressful situation. For example, the athlete in the above example would be engaging in emotion-focused coping if he or she used positive self-talk (e.g., "I am better trained than my opponent," "it doesn't matter whether I win over this opponent") to manage the feelings of anxiety aroused by competition against this particular opponent. Of course, problem-focused and emotion-focused coping can serve each other's goals. For example, if the athlete used the problem-focused strategy of avoiding the opponent, he or she would also have avoided the anxiety of competing against this person.

Similarly, Pearlin and Schooler (1978) classified coping into three categories: (1) responses that alter the meaning or appraisal of the stress, (2) responses that change the situation (problem-focused), and (3) responses intended to control distressed feelings (emotion-focused). Moos and colleagues (1983) classify coping behaviors according to both *method* and *focus*. *Method* of coping refers to whether the person deals with the stressful situation directly (for example, by making a plan of action and following it) or by avoiding the situation (for example, by refusing to believe that the situation exists). *Focus* of coping refers to whether efforts to manage stress attempt to change the way the person perceives the stressful situation, to change the situation itself (problem-focused), or to change the feelings that the situation evokes (emotion-focused).

Little empirical material has been reported on the specific coping behaviors of athletes (Feigley, 1985; Highlen & Bennett, 1983; Mahoney & Avener, 1977). Mahoney and Avener (1977) found that among elite gymnasts the better performers used more self-talk in both training and competition. Highlen and Bennett (1983) found similar results in a study of elite divers: those who qualified for the Pan American games used self-talk more in both training and competition than did nonqualifiers. Successful divers also thought less about their anxiety one hour before competition. During competition, qualifiers used more self-instructions and thought less about earlier mistakes than did nonqualifiers. Among wrestlers, qualifiers for the Pan American and World Championship teams blocked less of their anxiety than nonqualifiers one week before competition, and had fewer thoughts about the outcome of the tournament one hour before competition and during the competition (Higlen & Bennett, 1983).

Correlates of Coping Strategies   It seems axiomatic that different people cope with stress in different ways. One of our goals in this chapter is to assess whether there are patterns in the ways different athletes cope with the same stress, the Olympic trials. Previous researchers have identified patterns of coping in general population samples. Gender, age, education, and income were related to using specific coping behaviors when different sources of stress were considered (Billings & Moos, 1981; Holahan & Moos, 1987; Pearlin & Schooler, 1978).

Social Resources The term *social resources* refers to characteristics of social relationships, such as their number, type, structure, and quality (Moos & Mitchell, 1982). We address two kinds of social resources here: *social integration*, or the presence and number of relationships a person has, and *social support*, or the extent to which those relationships are emotionally supportive (House & Kahn, 1985). We differentiate between these two kinds of social resources because having relationships may matter in and of itself, but not all relationships are emotionally supportive (Turner, 1983).

Social resources are related to the kinds of behaviors people engage in to cope with stress (Thoits, 1986). For example, research with nonathletes found that being married (Billings & Moos, 1984; Moos, Brennan, Fondacaro & Moos, 1990) and having emotional support from one's family (Holahan & Moos, 1987) were related to the ways people coped with stress. In our study of Masters track and field athletes, we found that athletes who had emotionally supportive spouses were more likely to train with their spouses (Golding & Ungerleider, in press). We expected that some Olympians might report similar situations, and indeed, Don and Debbi Lawrence, husband and wife competitors and members of the 1988 U.S. Olympic Race Walking Team, told us:

> "We both train and compete as a couple . . . I think we are the first husband and wife team in race walking. We emphasize the team component because, in addition to competition, race walking is a way of life and our livelihood, too. We speak to youth about the importance of mutual support in relationships and the health benefits of our sport."

In our Masters study, athletes with emotionally supportive friends were more likely to train with their friends, whereas those with few friends were more likely to train alone (Golding & Ungerleider, in press). We also found that social resources had consequences for athletes' moods. When we considered social integration, we found that unmarried athletes were more depressed and confused, and athletes with fewer relatives were more anxious, angry, and confused, and less vigorous (Golding & Ungerleider, in press). Social support was also related to mood: athletes with unsupportive spouses were more depressed and less vigorous, those with less support from people at work had greater mood disturbance overall, those with unsupportive relatives were more angry, and those with unsupportive friends were less vigorous (Golding & Ungerleider, in press). We wondered how social resources would affect the ways in which elite athletes coped with the stress of competing in the Olympic Trials.

LITERATURE SUMMARY

Despite a lack of empirical results concerning athletes' coping behaviors, much has been written about athletic stress and how best to manage it (Buceta, 1985). It is somewhat surprising that so much emphasis has been placed on stress management, without the data on coping necessary as a guide for such work. We used data from the Elite Athlete Project to begin providing this kind of information. A more technical summary of these results is available elsewhere (Golding & Ungerleider, 1990).

RESULTS FROM THE ELITE ATHLETE PROJECT

Perceptions of Stress To make sense of the ways athletes coped with competing in the Olympic trials, it was necessary to understand the extent to which they perceived this event as stressful. To this end, we asked the athletes two questions. We developed the questions in consultation with a former Olympian and pilot-tested them with a group of ten additional former Olympians.

First, we asked "How much stress, if any, has this one sacrifice [the greatest sacrifice you have made in the past two years in order to train towards your Olympic goals] created for you?" We saw this question as corresponding loosely to perceptions of threat. On the average, the athletes saw the sacrifices they had made to train for the Olympics as moderately stressful, with about one-third choosing the "moderate" (middle) response category.

Second, we asked athletes, "How do you measure your level of commitment to making the United States Olympic team?" This question may be seen as loosely corresponding to perceptions of challenge. Vicki Huber, the 3,000 meter Olympian, commented on her commitment to training and making the team:

> "I think because it was the Olympics, such a huge goal, and just such an honor to be on the team, that I just worked so much harder for it. It was an obsession almost. I was not as nervous as I thought I was going to be because I don't think I had anything to lose. I was a twenty-one-year-old kid running the biggest race of my life, so what did I have to lose? I had made the finals, and that was all anybody ever thought I would do!"

On the average, athletes were somewhat more than moderately committed to making the team. Nearly one-third chose each of the highest and next-to-highest categories.

We wondered whether there were any patterns in which athletes perceived the trials as most stressful and which were most committed to success. When we considered personal characteristics, we found that men and younger athletes reported greater commitment to earning a place on the Olympic team. It is possible that on the average, men tended to have a more all-or-nothing attitude toward the trials, whereas women may have tended to take a more balanced approach, feeling that they had other sources of satisfaction in their lives. Another possibility is that traditional gender-role expectations resulted in men seeing athletic success as more important. Younger athletes may have been more committed because they may have estimated that their chances of being selected were greater. In any case, these tendencies refer to averages over a large group of individuals, and any individual might have greater or lesser commitment at different times.

When we considered athletic characteristics, we found that athletes who trained long hours perceived their sacrifices as relatively stressful, and reported greater commitment to making the team. It seems reasonable that long hours of training would result in greater stress because training would take time away from personal relationships, school, and occupational goals.

Long hours of training would also result in fatigue that would make it difficult to engage in these activities even when time was available. Other things being equal, athletes who trained longer did make a greater sacrifice in the sense that they sacrificed more time and energy, and a greater sacrifice appears to be experienced as more stressful.

At the same time, these athletes may have trained for many hours because of their prior commitment to their Olympic goals; or their perception of their own commitment may have changed as a result of their long training hours. The relation of training hours to commitment was especially strong for marathoners, which is not surprising in view of the length of their event compared to others'.

We also considered the role of other life stresses and athletic stresses, as measured by the SARRS (see chapter 5), in athletes' perception of the trials. Athletes who had experienced many of these events experienced greater stress in connection with sacrifices made to pursue Olympic goals. We speculated that this sense of threat occurred because the athletes felt that their coping resources were already partly depleted by the other stresses occurring in their lives.

Finally, we considered how social resources were related to the degree to which athletes experienced as stressful the sacrifices they made to reach the trials. As we mentioned earlier, we measured two kinds of social resources. We measured social integration by asking athletes whether they were married, whether they were employed, and how many friends and relatives they had kept in touch with in the six months before they completed the questionnaire. Unemployed athletes, particularly unemployed marathoners, reported being more committed to earning a position on the Olympic team, as did athletes with few friends. One possible explanation for this pattern is that athletes, especially those who must spend many hours training, give up jobs and friends out of a strong commitment to high-level achievement. Alternatively, it is possible that athletes with small social networks use commitment to individual achievement to substitute, in some sense, for social interaction (Golding & Ungerleider, in press). A third possible explanation for this pattern may be the athlete's relationship and obligation to corporate sponsors. Some competitors may feel a strong obligation to the financial reward system available to them if they succeed in their quest.

We measured emotional support with the Dimensions of Social Support Scale (Schaefer, Coyne & Lazarus, 1981). This scale assesses the emotional supportiveness of several people in the athlete's life: spouse, people at work, friends, relatives, and coach (the inclusion of coach was a modification for this study). Specifically, the questionnaire asks whether the person is reliable, shows caring toward the athlete, and is someone in whom the athlete can confide. Athletes with emotionally supportive work associates and coaches reported higher levels of commitment to earning a place on the Olympic team.

This result suggests that coaches who understand and have sensitivity toward the stress and mood swings of elite competitors may gain trust and mutual respect from their athletes, who in turn are willing to work harder and offer greater commitment. Athletes with emotionally supportive coaches were more likely to see the trials as challenging, but no more likely to see them as stressful. Informational support may also be important (House & Kahn, 1985). In discussing the importance of having a coach, Connie Price, the Olympic discus and shot put athlete, emphasized the importance of informational support:

> "It's important to have someone every now and then look at me. Especially in my discus, not so much in my shot, but in my discus, to make sure I am on target with my technique. I film myself and I can look at the tape, but sometimes it helps to have someone else . . . with an objective eye look at it too."

Coping Strategies We measured coping using Moos and colleagues' (1983) Health and Daily Living Form. The measure includes five scales assessing focus of coping.

When we examined patterns of personal characteristics that might be related to ways athletes coped with trials competition, we found that women were more likely than men to report information seeking, affective regulation, and emotional discharge. Studies of nonathletes have also found that women make greater use of information seeking (Moos et al. 1990; Pearlin & Schooler, 1978). We can attribute these gender differences to social expectations for women in general. Social norms encourage women, but not men, to ask others for help and to perceive and express their emotions (Spence & Helmreich, 1978). Thus, our data suggest that women athletes' behavior is consistent in some ways with these norms because these women cope with stress in much the same ways that society prescribes for all women. At the same time, because serious athletic participation is traditionally seen as a masculine activity (Porter & Foster, 1986; Reis & Jelsma, 1980), women athletes' behavior goes against society's norms for women.

We also found that more-educated respondents reported more logical analysis and problem solving. This pattern is consistent with past research on nonathletes (Billings & Moos, 1984) and with the assumption that formal education teaches rational, cognitive approaches to problems.

Athletes who trained for longer hours reported using more problem-solving strategies to cope with the stress of preparing for the trials. This finding makes sense because, to a point, spending extra hours training is often an excellent problem-solving strategy for an athlete trying to improve performance. Because athletes who used some problem-solving strategies tended to use the others, this also suggests that Olympic hopefuls who trained long hours were also likely to use other active, constructive approaches to dealing with the stress of competition.

Athletes who trained with a coach reported less logical analysis and more information seeking than those who did not. This result suggests two patterns of coping with the stress of preparing for the Olympic trials: one in which the athlete analyzes the situation logically on his or her own, and one in which the athlete tries to learn about ways to manage the situation, both from a coach and from other sources. The athlete might seek information because she or he has a coach available, since a coach would be an excellent source of information about ways to manage competitive stress. It is also possible that athletes who prefer to seek information will choose to train with a coach so that they can have this source of information available.

Women athletes who trained with a coach reported less affective regulation, on the average, than those who trained without a coach. One possible interpretation of this result is that training with a coach made the experience less distressing for these women, so they had fewer distressed feelings that they needed to manage. This interpretation is consistent with the theory that women tend to value personal relatedness more than men (Gilligan, 1983), and thus might be more comfortable coping with stress in an interpersonal context. Another possibility is that women who trained with a coach learned from their coaches ways to manage competitive stress other than expressing emotion.

When we examined the ways in which perception of the trials was related to the ways athletes coped with competing, we found some interesting patterns. Athletes who experienced their greatest sacrifice as highly stressful reported a greater degree of emotional expression as a way to manage the stress of competing in the trials. This result suggests that perceiving the trials as stressful was related to feeling and expressing distress. We might speculate that athletes who felt they had given up a lot to prepare for the trials, and therefore had the most to lose, found the training process most distressing.

On the other hand, athletes with greater commitment to making the U.S. team reported more logical analysis and problem solving than less-committed athletes. This pattern suggests active, positive attempts to cope with competitive stress. These coping strategies were related to better psychological outcomes in research on nonathletes (Billings & Moos, 1984), and might apply to athletes also. Because emotionally distressed athletes were less likely to make the team (see chapter 4), coping strategies related to emotional states are likely to be related to performance also. This result is important because our data suggest that when coaches are emotionally supportive, athletes tend to be more committed to making the team, and this commitment appears to be related to coping with the trials in ways that may promote positive emotional states, and ultimately, better performance.

The overall level of stress in the athletes' lives was also related to the way they managed the stress of the trials. Athletes under greater stress tended to use less intellectual or rationalized methods of coping (information seeking, affective regulation, and emotional discharge). Affective regulation and emotional discharge have been classified as emotion-focused (Billings & Moos, 1984). We speculated that this pattern occurs because the other stresses in the athlete's life evoke emotional distress, since stress is related to distressed mood (see chapter 5). This overall stress level appears to affect coping directly. It also seems to be related indirectly to coping, through influencing the athlete's perception of the stressfulness of the event. We saw above that athletes who were experiencing higher levels of stress from sources other than the trials tended to perceive the trials as more stressful. At the same time, emotional support, particularly from people at work, appeared to cancel out this tendency, decreasing emotion-focused coping.

Considering the solitary nature of track and field as a sport, a supportive social network would seem to be especially important to the track and field competitor. Unlike a sport such as football, where an individual is constantly surrounded by dozens of teammates and a large staff of coaches and trainers, most of these track and field athletes do not have such direct access to support. Olympian Jeff Atkinson shed some light on his personal social support network:

> "I would say that my mother definitely had an important impact on me; she got me going as far as some basic habits and patterns about how I view sports and life and training and so on. As far as the cliche, I'm going to win this one for her, I never had that sort of feeling, but rather, you might say that I had some sense of mortality at a fairly young age. I was determined to basically do the best that I could in a whole lot of things, including studies and track. And as I got older, I felt a strong bond with my runner friends because this is now part of my social support system."

Personal, athletic, and social characteristics are clearly associated with different styles of coping with athletic stress. At the same time, these associations refer to averages over very large groups of elite athletes, and what works well for one athlete may not work well for another, even if their personal and athletic characteristics are similar. It is important that athletes and those who work with them find the ways of coping that are most effective for the individual athlete. Understanding and appreciating these individual differences may help coaches and sport consultants identify athletes at risk, or those needing assistance with specific interventions when facing competitive stress.

SUMMARY—IMPLICATIONS AND APPLICATIONS

Olympian Earl Bell described one way in which he copes with competitive stress:

> "One thing I think I'm probably pretty good about, is sticking to my own expectations of myself instead of freaking out about what other people are doing around me in the competition. I pretty much have a game plan and a goal and expect a certain thing out of myself on a certain day. Whether somebody jumps three feet higher or three feet lower doesn't really matter. I basically set my goal and accomplish it for the day . . . if I jump higher, well that's fine too. I call that the *let it happen attitude!*"

We think that this "let it happen attitude" is likely to be especially effective for many track and field athletes. Unlike competitors in some other sports (e.g., wrestling, boxing, football), track and field athletes have direct control over their own performances, but not over others'. No matter how skilled the sprinter, long jumper, or discus thrower, that athlete can do very little to affect the performance of a competitor. Therefore, concentrating on the elements of one's own performance, rather than using mental energy worrying about how an opponent might do, would be a good problem-focused approach to competitive anxiety. Useful emotion-focused efforts might include admitting to oneself: "there is really nothing (within the rules!) I can do to increase my chances of winning except focus on my own race, throws, jumps, etc . . . " Research consistent with this recommendation comes from a study of elite divers, in which, one hour before competition, qualifiers thought less about their opponents and more positively about their own performance than did nonqualifiers (Highlen & Bennett, 1983).

There is no one "magic bullet," no one coping method or resource, that will successfully serve all individuals across all situations. The more diverse a person's repertoire of coping skills and resources, the better. Three thousand meter Olympian PattiSue Plumer noted some of the benefits of diversity in coping with injury:

"Yes, I cross-trained a lot. I swam a lot! I did some biking, some weight lifting, and a lot of walking. I swam with the cast on. . . . It really made me change my life actually quite a bit, because I decided after that to go to law school. Before that I decided to just concentrate on running. I graduated from college and I was really concentrating on running. And two months later I broke my leg, and there I was, stuck. And I realized that probably it wasn't a good idea to put all your eggs in one basket, so to speak. Basically that's my philosophy in life. If something's not working out I try to fix it, and if it doesn't fix, then I do something else."

Olympic gold and bronze medalist Danny Everett also emphasized the importance of an individualized approach:

"You have to be patient and accomplish your own goals. Don't try and accomplish anyone else's goals . . . you need to take small steps one at a time and not big strides that fulfill other people's expectations!"

References

Billings, A. G., & Moos. R. H. (1981). The role of coping responses and social resources in attenuating the stress of life events. *Journal of Behavioral Medicine, 4,* 139–57.

Billings, A. G., & Moos, R. H. (1984). Coping, stress, and social resources among adults with unipolar depression. *Journal of Personality and Social Psychology, 46,* 877–91.

Bramwell, S. T., Masuda, M., Wagner, N. N., & Holmes, T. H. (1975). Psychological factors in athletic injuries: Development and application of the Social and Athletic Readjustment Rating Scale (SARRS). *Journal of Human Stress, 1,* 6–20.

Brown, G. W., & Harris, T. (1978). *Social origins of depression* New York: Free Press.

Buceta, J. M. (1985). Some guidelines for the prevention of excessive stress in athletes. *International Journal of Sport Psychology, 16,* 46–58.

Feigley, D. A. (1985). Coping with fear in high level gymnastics. In J. H. Salmela, B. Petiot, & T. B. Hoshizaki (Eds.), *Psychological nurturing and guidance of gymnastic talent* (pp. 13–27). Montreal: Sport Psyche Editions, 1987.

Gilligan, C. (1983). *In a different voice.* Cambridge, MA: Harvard University Press.

Golding, J. M., & Ungerleider, S. (in press). Social resources and mood among Masters track and field athletes. *Journal of Applied Sport Psychology.*

Golding, J. M., & Ungerleider, S. (1990). *Coping with the stress of Olympic competition.* Unpublished manuscript, University of California, San Francisco.

Grimsley, J. R., & Bunn, W. H. (1987, November). Anxiety and stress in athletic performance. *Texas Coach,* pp. 28–30

Higlen, P. S., & Bennett, B. B. (1983). Elite divers and wrestlers: A comparison between open and closed skill athletes. *Journal of Sport Psychology, 5,* 390–409.

Holahan, C. J., & Moos, R. H. (1987). Personal and contextual determinants of coping strategies. *Journal of Personality and Social Psychology, 52,* 946–55.

House, J. S., & Kahn, R. L (1985). Measures and concepts of social support. In S. Cohen & S. L. Syme (Eds.), *Social support and health* (pp. 83–108). Orlando: Academic Press.

Kanner, A. D., Coyne, J. C., Schaefer, C., & Lazarus, R. S. (1981). Comparison of two modes of stress measurement: Daily hassles and uplifts versus major life events. *Journal of Behavioral Medicine, 4,* 1–39.

Lazarus, R. S., & Folkman, S. (1984). *Stress, appraisal, and coping.* New York: Springer.

Lloyd, C. (1980). Life events and depressive disorders reviewed: II. Events as precipitating factors. *Archives of General Psychiatry, 37,* 541–48.

Mahoney, M. J., & Avener, M. (1977). Psychology of the elite athlete: An exploratory study. *Cognitive Therapy and Research, 1,* 135–41.

Martens, R. (1977). *Sport competition anxiety test.* Champaign, IL: Human Kinetics.

May, J. R., & Sieb, G. E. (1987). Athletic injuries: Psychosocial factors in the onset, sequelae, rehabilitation, and prevention. In J. R. May & M. J. Asken (Eds.), *Sport psychology* (pp. 157–85). New York: PMA Publishing.

Moos, R. H., Brennan, P. L., Fondacaro, M. R., & Moos, B. S. (1990). Approach and avoidance coping responses among older problem and non-problem drinkers. *Psychology and Aging, 5,* 31–40.

Moos, R. H., Cronkite, R. C., Billings, A. G., & Finney, J. W. (1983). *Health and daily living form manual.* Palo Alto, CA: Social Ecology Laboratory, Veterans Administration and Stanford University Medical Center.

Moos, R. H., & Mitchell, R. E. (1982). Social network resources and adaptation: A conceptual framework. In T. A. Wills (Ed.), *Basic processes in helping relationships* (pp. 213–23). New York: Academic Press.

Murphy, P. (1986). Stress and the athlete: Coping with exercise. *The Physician and Sportsmedicine, 14,* 141–46.

Pearlin, L. I., & Schooler, C. (1978). The structure of coping. *Journal of Health and Social Behavior, 19,* 2–21.

Porter, K., & Foster, J. (1986). *The mental athlete: Inner training for peak performance.* Dubuque, IA: Wm. C. Brown.

Reis, H., & Jelsma, B. (1980). A social psychology of sex differences in sport. In W. F. Straub (Ed.), *Sport psychology: An analysis of athlete behavior* (2nd ed.) (pp. 276–86). Ithaca, NY: Movement Publications.

Scanlon, T. K. (1984). Competitive stress and the child athlete. In J. M. Silva & R. S. Weinberg (Eds.), *Psychological foundations of sport* (pp. 118–29). Champaign, IL: Human Kinetics.

Schaefer, C., Coyne, J., & Lazarus, R. (1981). The health-related functions of social support. *Journal of Behavioral Medicine, 4,* 381–405.

Smith, R. E. (1980). A cognitive-affective approach to stress management training for athletes. In C. Nadeau, W. Halliwell, K. Newell, & G. Roberts (Eds.), *Psychology of motor behavior and sport* (pp. 54–73). Champaign, IL: Human Kinetics.

Smith, R. E. (1986). Toward a cognitive-affective model of athletic burnout. *Journal of Sport Psychology, 8,* 36–50.

Spence, J. T., & Helmreich, R. L. (1978). *Masculinity and femininity: Their psychological dimensions, correlates, and antecedents.* Austin: University of Texas Press.

Stafford, C. (1984). Coping with the pressure. *Canadian Skater, 11,* (3), 29–30.

Thoits, P. A. (1986). Social support as coping assistance. *Journal of Consulting and Clinical Psychology, 54,* 416–23.

Turner, R. J. (1983). Direct, indirect, and moderating effects of social support upon psychological distress and associated conditions. In H. B. Kaplan (Ed.), *Psychological stress: Trends in theory and research.* New York: Academic Press.

Weiss, M. R., & Troxel, R. K. (1986). Psychology of the injured athlete. *Athletic Training, 21,* (2), 104–9, 154.

CHAPTER 7

"I believe that deals are cut all the time with federations and national governing bodies, and that the big gun athletes . . . the big world record holders and the medalists get passed over in the drug testing . . . so that no scandals take place. That's probably one of the biggest reasons I was shocked when Ben got caught. I said to myself *MY GOD . . . THEY CAUGHT A WORLD RECORD HOLDER IN THE SPRINTS . . . THEY CAUGHT THE STAR OF THE OLYMPICS!!!* I couldn't believe HE got caught. I thought somebody should have gotten him off or something. He's the biggest person in track and field history. That's when all the rumors started flying around, it got really messy."

(Anonymous athlete)

Substance Use, Abuse, and Athletic Myths

Michael Cooper, the former outstanding NBA star of the Los Angeles Lakers, noted several years ago in a postgame interview:

> "I don't think we will ever have the serious problem of drug abuse found in places around the NBA and in other franchises. . . . It's not that we aren't capable of having problems, we are human like all the other athletes, it's just that we know each other well as individuals and as team players . . . and if anybody on the Laker team were in trouble, you know messing around with coke or something, we would all be sensitive to it and we would confront that person and offer the necessary support for help."

Cooper's comments were made some two years before the Seoul games. Since 1986, we have learned of the tragic drug-related deaths of Len Bias, George Rogers, and other professional competitors, all great athletes in the prime of their careers and their lives (Burt, 1987). In the wake of these deaths, most sports officials attributed their drug and alcohol excesses to isolated cases of athletes out of control and overly indulgent. Then, in the 1988 Olympic Games in Seoul, nine Olympians were disqualified for testing positive for anabolic steroids. Ben Johnson, the talented Canadian sprinter, was also sent home in disgrace after testing positive for a performance enhancing drug, stripped of a gold medal in the 100 meters, banned from Canadian athletics, and suspended for two years from Olympic competition.

DRUGS IN SPORTS: PAST, PRESENT, AND FUTURE

"A lot of people are using performance enhancers and a lot of people are just brave enough to say yes, sure, if you're going to win, you're going to have to use drugs, and you're going to have to blood dope. I think that there probably are a very few great, great, athletes who don't have to. But across the board, I think that anyone who sets world records, wins gold medals, probably has been using banned substances" (Anonymous athlete).

Editor's Note: No empirical survey data were collected for this chapter. Because of the highly charged atmosphere surrounding substance abuse and performance enhancement, The Athletics Congress was unwilling to allow measures assessing prevalence of drug use. Likewise, all quotes from 1988 Olympians found in the text are anonymous to protect the confidentially of U.S. athletes.

Probably the most devastating outcome from the disclosure that Ben Johnson tested positive for stanozolol, an anabolic steroid, was that a lot of people knew it. His coach, doctor, trainer, and a lot of his colleagues in Canada and the U.S. knew that Johnson was using performance enhancing drugs and that it was just a matter of time before he got caught. Steroids have been the "breakfast of champions" among athletes for many years. Most professionals in sport science who work with athletes have known this fact for a long time (Almond, Cart & Harvey, 1984; Johnson & Moore, 1988).

The 1988 Olympic Games set the stage for a drug drama to be played out with full media attention and a confrontation in an international forum. One could say that the unfortunate loss for Mr. Johnson was a blessing in disguise for other athletes. In addition to Johnson, members of the Bulgarian and Hungarian weight lifting teams turned up positive. To relieve further embarrassment, both teams left Seoul and returned home during the games. A British athlete testing positive for the banned substance pseudoephedrine, was not disqualified because he had very small traces of it in his urine. According to Dr. Park Jong Sei, the director of the Olympic drug testing lab in Seoul, "as many as twenty athletes at the games turned up positive but were not disqualified". This comment led to rumors and speculations that many other athletes were using drugs and getting away with it. Dr. Robert Voy, the former chief medical officer for the USOC, noted that more than half of the 9,000 athletes at the games had used steroids at some point in their training (Janofsky & Alfano, 1988). Additionally one Olympian told us:

"My belief is that if I had to take an estimate, about sixty-five percent of the top five, let's say top ten in the world in every event, are doing something illegal. That basically is the growth hormones in the ballistic events and blood doping for the distance events. I think all of the major distance runners that have really run incredible times are blood doping. I think the middle distance runners are using a combination of blood doping and steroids" (Anonymous athlete).

The history of substance abuse in elite sport competition, including the illegal use of steroids, is well documented. The following is an overview (Almond et al. 1984; Beckett & Cowan, 1979; Clarke, 1984; Coward, 1987; Cramer, 1985; Goldman, 1984; Percy, 1980; Tricker & Cook, 1990; Ryan, 1984).

- In 1904, Tom Hanks won the marathon in the St. Louis Olympics and subsequently lapsed into a coma. He had ingested brandy and strychnine before the race.
- In 1952, a cyclist died during the Helsinki Olympics after using amphetamines and coffee.
- In 1957, the American Medical Association appointed a special commission to look at the abuse of amphetamines in elite athletics.
- In 1958, a survey conducted by the American College of Sports Medicine found that more than 35% of a sample of 441 coaches recommended the amphetamine Benzedrine.
- In 1960, at the Rome Olympics, a Danish cyclist died of a mixture of amphetamines and alcohol and a sprint athlete died of a heroin overdose.
- In 1962, the IOC passed the first resolution against "doping."
- In 1967, the IOC established a medical commission to control drug use.
- In 1968, after announcing the first drug testing program at the Mexico City Olympics, Col. F. Don Miller of the USOC noted, "we must obliterate the image of the chemical athlete."
- In 1970, a survey of ninety-three professional athletes on thirteen NFL teams revealed that 61% used amphetamines.
- In 1972, at the Munich Olympics, American swimmer Rick De-Mott was disqualified and lost his gold medal for using a prescription drug indicated for asthma.
- In 1974, at the British Commonwealth Games, 16.4% of the athletes sampled tested positive for a banned substance.
- In 1976, prior to the Montreal Games, seven U.S. swimmers tested positive for banned substances. At the games a few months later, 2.9% of those tested were positive, including two athletes who won gold medals and one who was a silver medalist.
- In 1976, Norway implemented the first random testing year round, including a comprehensive education, intervention, and treatment program.

- In 1983, at the Pan American Games, seventeen athletes (including two from the U.S.) were disqualified for using anabolic steroids. Eleven U.S. athletes decided not to submit to testing and withdrew from competition.
- In 1984, after the Los Angeles Olympics, eight U.S. cyclists admitted that they had "blood doped," or stored their blood and re-infused it prior to competition.
- In 1984, the publication of *Death In The Locker Room* (Goldman, 1984) reported eleven deaths and fourteen cases of liver cancer among athletes using steroids.
- In 1985, a NCAA survey of 2,000 college athletes from eleven schools revealed that 27% of respondents use marijuana, 12% use cocaine, 11% use major pain killers, and 82% use alcohol frequently.
- At the Seoul Games, in addition to Ben Johnson, eight other athletes tested positive and were disqualified. Both the Hungarian and Bulgarian weight lifting teams withdrew from competition and went home.
- A breakdown of chemicals used at the 1988 games revealed that those testing positive had used anabolic steroids, diuretics, amphetamines, beta blockers, and high levels of caffeine.
- In testimony before the Senate Judiciary Committee in April 1989, a former Olympian and present coach testified that some twenty U.S. track and field athletes had been using steroids to prepare for the 1988 Olympics. Another prominent athlete testified that two of our gold medalists at Seoul had used banned substances.
- In October 1989, the executive board of the USOC approved the most comprehensive random drug testing program ever implemented. The program includes an outside auditor and coordinates the forty-one national governing bodies of individual sports.
- In the fall of 1989, the USOC and the Soviet Union agreed to a mutual testing program, including a worldwide computer system to track athletes' test results.

ORIGINS OF SUBSTANCE ABUSE

What are the causes of substance abuse among athletes? Many scientists point to status, peer pressure, boredom, and performance enhancement as the most common reasons for drug use (Beckett & Cowan, 1979; Voy, 1986). Substance abuse among athletes typically occurs in the context of an ethic that is perpetrated early on when an athlete shows promise in junior and senior high school. This ethic is one of special treatment as early as seventh grade. Athletic skills are valued by society, and consequently, athletes receive special attention, grades, and social benefits. Athletes go through life with a distorted view of their own self-image and self-worth. From grade school to the professional ranks, athletes live by a different code of social behavior, one that involves playing by a different set of societal rules and mores. Scholar athletes are heavily recruited (even from one high school to another), promised academic security blankets with fringe benefits, and special treatment (Penn, 1988; Ungerleider, 1986).

We can imagine this ethic having at least two consequences. The first consequence relates to difficulties faced by athletes and nonathletes alike, that are intensified for athletes. Athletes are pampered in college, and often coping skills are not developed to handle the pressures of academia and other responsibilities. Athletes may use alcohol or other drugs in an attempt to cope with the stresses of day-to-day life—and may be at higher risk for this maladaptive coping because of the ethic overvaluing athletes and the resulting pampering. If the athlete excels and moves into Olympic and/or professional stature, there is even further alienation from society. The athlete is put on a pedestal of hero worship. This situation may place athletes at risk for not adequately developing refusal and social skills, with the result that substance abuse promoted by peer pressure or boredom may be difficult to resist. Thus, athletes appear to be at risk for the same kinds of substance abuse problems as other people, especially other young people, but more so because of the special circumstances involved in being an athlete (Caudill, Kantor & Ungerleider, 1990; Chappell, 1987; Pentz et al. 1985; Ungerleider, 1986; Ungerleider & Caudill, in press).

A second consequence of the overvaluing of athletes by others is an overemphasis by athletes themselves on performance enhancement. The desire to enhance performance is specific to athletes, rather than being a general problem of people in this age range (unless we count drug use related to a desire to enhance other kinds of performance, such as use of stimulants to study all night). Research from college athletics has shown that predictors of alcohol and other drug use include peer use, failure in academic achievement, environmental and media pressure, and family dysfunction (Bloch & Ungerleider, 1987). The 1985 NCAA University of Michigan study (Anderson & McKeag, 1985) found that:

- student athletes use alcohol and drugs more frequently with friends than with teammates;
- major sources for obtaining illegal drugs are friends, relatives and "other" nonteammate sources;
- with the exception of cocaine, the majority of student athletes begin their use of alcohol and other drugs in high school or before;
- many coaches and trainers are illegally dispensing ergogenic drugs;
- major sources of anabolic steroids are from nonteam related sources.

According to one Olympian:

> "I just think the effects of steroids, from what I've heard, are physically debilitating—I mean, they will eventually kill you. But I still think there are some people that would go ahead and use them, just because of the short-term benefits of getting that fame and fortune. And I think a lot of athletes, well some athletes, have done that, just to get that short-term prestige, make that money, do it for a year or two, and then get out of the sport. Hell, I'd do it for a few years, just to get what I could out of it" (Anonymous athlete).

Sports Illustrated reported the results of a survey which asked athletes whether they would take a drug that guaranteed them a gold medal but would kill them within a week after winning, and 50% responded affirmatively! This situation appears to reflect an overvaluing of athletic performance to the point that, in athletes' minds, winning is worth the grave damage to their mental, physical, and social well-being that results from drug abuse. As a commentary on this situation, George Vecsey (1984), sports analyst for the *New York Times,* noted that unethical tactics by coaches and boosters are as dangerous in a social sense as drugs are in a medical sense. College athletics, which began as recreation for legitimate students, has become a monster that requires full-time surveillance, not unlike the local drug dealers. This news commentary was in response to 107 ethical violations charged by the NCAA to a well-known football power on the east coast.

CATEGORIES OF SUBSTANCE USE

Drugs are used in sport to increase strength, endurance, and speed; decrease fatigue, pain, and anxiety; and enhance aggression, attention, and concentration. Drugs used in the athletic environment can be classified into eight categories: stimulants, depressants, analgesics, beta blockers, diuretics, human growth hormone, blood doping, and anabolic steroids (American College of Sports Medicine, 1984; *Physicians' Desk Reference,* 1990; U.S. Department of Justice, 1988).

Stimulants

Stimulants are probably the most widely used drugs among elite competitors. Stimulants include amphetamines such as cocaine, methamphetamine, methylphenidate, and diet drugs such as diethylpropion and phenmetrazine. Stimulants also include epinephrine-type drugs such as ephedrine, etafedrine, and isoprenaline which are commonly prescribed for asthma and bronchial distress. Strychnine is a commonly abused stimulant with serious and sometimes fatal side effects. Benzphetamine is also known to be used to increase arousal and concentration. Caffeine, the most widely used stimulant among society at large, is now on the banned substance list at twelve micrograms per milliliter of urine. In our study of Olympic track and field participants, nearly one-half of the sample reported never drinking coffee while only three athletes were at the other extreme, drinking five to six cups daily. Nicotine is not a banned substance but does possess stimulant characteristics that produce epinephrine releases from the adrenal glands. In our study of elite athletes, we found that nearly all athletes reported no tobacco use with the exception of four athletes who smoke regularly. Athletic benefits reported from the use of stimulants are increased alertness, faster response time, better motivation. The side effects are also well-known, including depression, fatigue, and irritability. Increased use can lead to hyperaggressiveness and psychotic behavior (Mandell, 1979). The long-term consequences are psychological and physiological addiction.

Depressants

Probably the most widely known and most abused depressant is alcohol. Elite athletes in our study seemed to be equally as prudent with their alcohol intake as their caffeine use. One-third never drank wine. Two-thirds reported drinking wine from one to four times a week, and only one athlete reported daily consumption. A third of the sample never drank beer. Two-thirds reported drinking beer between one and four times a week, while seven athletes imbibed daily. Nearly two-thirds of the sample never drank hard alcohol. Other types of depressants include barbiturates and sedative hypnotics such as Amytal, Butisol, Nembutal, Seconal, and Tuinal which are commonly used to treat insomnia. Another category of depressants is antianxiety drugs. These include the benzodiazepines like Dalmane, Valium, Librium, Serax, Tranxene, and Halcion.

These drugs are not on the banned substance list because, in part, they typically hinder performance rather than improve it. Two reasons athletes abuse these drugs are that society provides a good environmental support system for alcohol, including the use of alcohol while driving and having a good time. Second, alcohol and other depressants allow the athlete to "come down" from intense competition and provide a "tranquility" effect. The depressants are also known as disinhibitors, whereby fear and anxiety may be decreased while risk-taking behaviors can be accelerated. The downside of alcohol abuse is well-known in both the research literature and daily media. What is less known is the psychological and physical dependence that depressants, including alcohol, carry with them.

Narcotic and Non-Narcotic Analgesics

Both narcotic and non-narcotic drugs are used for relief of pain during the healing and rehabilitation process. Unfortunately, they are also used in the emotional pain reduction process as well. The narcotic analgesics include codeine, Darvon, Demerol, Dilaudid, morphine, Percodan, Talwin, and Vicodin. Narcotic analgesics can cause adverse reactions such as depression of breathing, nausea, vomiting, constipation, cardiovascular depression, and death by overdose. Other dangers are well-known to physicians who might inject an athlete for temporary relief of pain during a serious injury so that the athlete can then compete. The athlete competes, absent of pain, and then returns to the training table with more severe tissue damage. The non-narcotic analgesics include Tylenol, Anaprox, aspirin, Dolobid, ibuprofen, Nalfon, Suprol, Butazolidin, and Indocin. All of these drugs relieve pain, inflammation, and swelling, and some are available over the counter. The serious problem with abuse comes when athletes become their own doctors and self-prescribe. Although these drugs are not habit-forming, known side effects include shortness of breath, rash, itching, gastrointestinal distress, and impaired kidney functions.

Beta Blockers

Beta blockers are commonly used to lower blood pressure and heart rate, and block sympathetic nervous system activity. Shooters, archers, ski jumpers, dancers, and gymnasts have been known to use these drugs to "quiet the system" prior to competition. Beta blockers include Inderal, Lopressor, Normozide, Sectral, and Timolide. For longer duration sports the beta blockers hamper performance because of slowed reactions and onset of fatigue. The most common abuse of these substances has been in shooting events, including the biathlon.

Diuretics

Diuretics have caused considerable concern, especially in the last two Olympiads. Diuretics, which remove water from the body, are used for quick weight loss and have major implications for wrestlers and boxers trying to perform in a particular class or weight category. Diuretics include Chlorithiazide, metolazone, spironolactone, and triamterene. One well-known diuretic which caused several disqualifications in Seoul is furosemide. Side effects to abuse of these drugs include muscle weakness, gastric irritation, light-headedness, dizziness, muscle spasm, transient blurred vision, and headaches.

Human Growth Hormone

The use of human growth hormone as a method of performance enhancement falls into a category of its own. This drug offers the same effect as steroids but at present is not detectable in IOC labs. Traditionally, the human growth hormone is used for children with very serious growth deficiencies. Its use has been limited (as far as researchers know) because of its availability. Its only available source is the pituitary glands of cadavers, with several glands needed to make up a significant dose. Manufacturers of HGH note that on the black market prices are in excess of $2,000 for a single dose (Neff, 1989). One of the side effects reported in the literature is acromegaly, an overgrowth of bones in the feet, hands, forehead, nose, and jaw (Zemper, 1991). The side effects and limited availability have apparently kept this drug out of the limelight for now.

Blood Doping

Blood doping has become quite prominent in recent years, especially among endurance athletes. This procedure consists of removing two pints of blood from the athlete several weeks before competition, freezing the blood, and then reinfusing the fresh blood just prior to the event. During the replacement period, the body produces new red blood cells to replace those withdrawn. The reinfusion of the stored blood offers additional red blood cells and the effect of increasing oxygen supplies to the blood. This has been reported to be an enhancement in run-

ning, swimming, cross-country skiing, and cycling. The increase
in aerobic capacity may give the athlete a competitive edge. The
risks of reinfusing blood under unsupervised conditions are infection and disease. Infusing someone else's blood (which was
reported during the 1984 games) becomes a greater hazard. Adverse reactions may be found in the incompatibility of blood
type as well as risk of hepatitis, HIV infection, and other fatal
diseases. There is currently no reliable test for blood doping, although researchers in Europe are experimenting with a procedure (Zemper, 1991).

Anabolic Steroids

Probably the most widely discussed topic in this area since the
fall of 1988 is the abuse of anabolic steroids for performance
enhancement. This group of drugs increases the use of
androgen (male hormone) and decreases estrogen (female hormone) levels in the body. Steroid use may result in deterioration
of vital organs such as the liver, kidneys, and reproductive organs (Kleiner et al. 1989; Lamb, 1984). It is reported anecdotally
that muscles do get bigger, body weight increases and that
some weight lifters improve their performance. It was clear to
the casual observer in Seoul, South Korea, that Ben Johnson's
body mass had changed significantly over the two years before
the Olympics (Shorter, 1988). According to the American College of Sports Medicine (1984), "there is no scientific evidence
that anabolic steriods either aid or hinder athletic performance."
Weight gain and tissue enlargement are symptoms that usually
suggest steroid use but not necessarily greater performance. Researchers at Case Western Reserve Medical School found that
steroid users in their clinical study had lipoprotein profiles in-
dicative of a very high risk of heart disease (Kleiner et al.,
1989). Under the best of clinical conditions, steroid use appears
to have serious long-term effects. More serious, however, is the
finding that self-administration of steroids reported among some
weight lifting athletes is reported to be eight times the recommended dose (Burkett & Falduto, 1984; Altman, 1988; Tenant,
Black & Voy, 1988). Even in controlled settings, the following
adverse reactions have been found: increased risks of liver disease, cancer, decreased immune function, kidney stones and

gallstones, hypertension, prostate enlargement, testicular atrophy, sterility, impotence, swelling of men's breasts, anaphylactic shock, stunted growth in adolescents, clitoris enlargement, hirsutism, male baldness, breast reduction, and fetal damage (Goldman, 1985; Kleiner et al., 1989).

Sports Illustrated reported just twenty-four hours after his IOC drug test that Ben Johnson had been injecting stanozolol so often that his liver was seriously affected (Johnson & Moore, 1988). Nearly a year after the Seoul games, Mr. Johnson testified before the United States House of Representatives in Washington, D.C., in support of a bill to tighten controls on steroids. During his testimony he noted that since taking steroids in 1981 he had serious problems with his liver, "I was lucky, I got caught in time" (Janofsky, 1989). One study of athletes found a manic-depressive disorder diagnosed for 22% of the athletes using steroids, while 12% showed psychotic symptoms. Athletes in all cases displayed major emotional and physiological withdrawal when the steroids were terminated (Pope & Katz, 1988).

EDUCATION

One U.S. Olympian told us:

> "It just wasn't that big of a deal. And I didn't think that it was a problem internationally. I thought that it wasn't a problem necessarily for the sport until I saw and heard about high school kids using steroids to get big so that they could, you know, impress people. And I see that as a real abuse. Up until then—I just felt that there wasn't a drug abuse problem at the top level" (Anonymous athlete).

It is important for coaches, trainers, and medical personnel to be knowledgeable about drug-related complications, the myths related to steroid use, and the ethical, moral, and legal complications involved. According to Dr. Harmon Brown, chair of The Athletic Congress' Sports Medicine Committee, the widespread use of steroids, from junior high to elite male and female athletes, has been known to the sports medicine community for some time. It is a concern that is just *now* starting to permeate the general medical community and field of endocrinology. Brown notes that a major source of anabolic steroids "is still through prescription by health professionals" (Brown, 1989). He also states that the statistics are quite grim: 6.6% of male high school students in America use steroids, suggesting a user pool of 250,000 to 500,000 young people; 38% of those youngsters began using by age fifteen; 57% report using steroids to enhance performance while 35% report using steroids to "look good." Most alarming, however, is that among high school users, 20% receive their steroids from medical doctors, pharmacists, or veterinarians. In some cases, the credibility of the medical community has been challenged by reports that steroids alter body mass and increase strength, especially for weight and power sports. Educational programs will have to overcome peer pressure and some medical myths to combat the prolific use of steroids in sports.

TESTING PROCEDURES AND CONTROL EFFORTS

One of our American athletes noted:

> "There are many stories I can tell you, like competing against several people from the Soviet bloc, and it was fifty-eight minutes after I was supposed to be called to be tested. I got fourth, and they called me to be tested. What happened to the other people? What happened to first, second, and third? You know, they don't normally test fourth when there's a world record holder in the meet. So, you don't know what kind of deals are made. I think they went down the line until they found somebody they could test" (Anonymous athlete).

The issues that arose from the Seoul 1988 Games are now being addressed in a systematic and, hopefully, productive direction. The IOC, in collaboration with national governing bodies from around the globe, are looking at how best to deal with rampant substance abuse. For the first time, policies are being set forth that outline consequences for using performance enhancing drugs. Random drug testing will now be conducted at the local level so that athletes do not "slip through the cracks" and end up in international competition only to be tested positive and then disqualified. Random testing for drug use will be conducted year-round, including non-Olympic years, so athletes who might experiment with drugs and then taper off before the Olympics will be discouraged from starting. Also, random testing will be conducted between nations so each governing body can observe whether there is fair play across continents. In addition, the penalties for using and distributing banned substances will be greater than ever. Coaches, trainers, and medical personnel will be asked to participate in identifying substance users and then follow up with appropriate measures (Brown, 1989; Duda, 1984; Janofsky, 1988).

Problems at U.S. Headquarters   One Olympian told us:

> "There's a whole lot of cover-up. As far as TAC is concerned, there's been documented evidence that they've pushed a lot of things under the rug for a number of years. Where people have tested positive they let them slide. I don't know if it's documented for the public, but it's documented. I don't know if it's going to come out or not. I think there's too many privacy issues involved here. Lack of due process and that sort of thing. In other words, you can't publicize this information now when the samples are gone and no one can verify it. For instance there are letters that are transcribed which have said something to the effect that we don't want to process these urine samples. We don't know who they belong to, or we may know who they belong to, but they were never processed, so we can't publicize it. Mr. or Ms. athlete tested positive for testosterone at such-and-such a meet, when he/she never had a chance to prove or disprove that in any kind of hearing or procedure" (Anonymous athlete).

Others have also identified problems at The Athletic Congress, the governing body for track and field (Voy, 1990). A major reorganization and reshuffling of key personnel is being called for as of this writing. The random testing has come under intense scrutiny, and athletes are now calling for radical change.

> "The testing procedure must be totally autonomous, conducted by an independent board, outside of TAC, or perhaps an independent accounting firm. If they can handle the Academy Awards, they can probably handle us!" (Anonymous athlete).

PROFESSIONAL VS. AMATEUR ATHLETICS

Part of the problem with TAC appears to be public relations and promotions. Athletes compare their governing body to the NFL or the NBA and perceive the TAC staff as inadequate to meet the demands of a professional organization. Part of the problem at TAC, articulated by several elite athletes, is that the entire organization, including the drug testing component, has gone from being an amateur mom-and-pop organization to a highly complex professional sports organization. At the elite level, this is a profession with thousands of athletes and an antiquated administration staffed by volunteers. According to some athletes, it appears as if TAC wants the professional benefits, but they don't want the professional responsibility and liability. TAC needs to reassess their priorities and understand that competent management has to be a top-down effort not dissimilar to professional sports franchises. Part of that responsibility will have to include a professional marketing organization and professional public relations experts. TAC must realize that they are an industry; a sports and entertainment industry, with a lot of responsibility to their constituency and the public at large. They are a profession. And in the same way that professional lawyers are governed, from the little storefront lawyer all the way up to the Wall Street megafirms, elite athletes have to abide by certain minimum standards of conduct.

PREVENTION AND INTERVENTION STRATEGIES

Most Olympic drug testing experts are convinced that the "athletic drug wars" will never be won by high tech, sophisticated, gas chromatography or mass spectroscopy testing equipment. According to one expert, Dr. Donald Catlin of UCLA, most athletes already know more than the medical specialists (Janofsky & Alfano, 1988). They have already learned how to circumvent the system by using masking agents which slow excretion rates to undetectable levels. New steroids are already on the black market which have not been identified in a metabolite pattern by testing procedures and could be invisible to the screening process (Zemper, 1991). Random testing appears to be only a short-term deterrence effort. Major deterrence efforts must include a nationwide awareness program involving community-based support from corporations, schools, mental health agencies, and other key players in the private sector (Ungerleider & Bloch, 1987; 1988).

Prevention, education, and intervention strategies affecting the demand side of drug use (as opposed to supply side) will need to be part of the strategy. Education and prevention efforts must begin at the primary school level in conjunction with K-12 health curricula, D.A.R.E. programs, "Just Say No Clubs," Reach America, Project IMPACT, and other prevention strategies. These programs must collaborate with coaches, administrators, and schools to continue training in prevention, early intervention, and identification of substance use. Prevention and intervention strategies must be paired with deterrence and testing procedures to provide a comprehensive community-based model which will then have an opportunity to affect this serious social problem (Pentz, 1985; Ungerleider & Caudill, in press).

One of our Olympians noted:

> "The research, the complexity of all the things that go into developing a top-level athlete, there are so many things. They're so complex that you put something like anabolic steroids in the formula, and it just becomes another piece of the puzzle. And the preparation and the activities involved in becoming a top-level athlete, they're so abnormal. The things that you do to yourself are so abnormal to begin with that perhaps using a synthetic hormone isn't that much different than other things that you're doing" (Anonymous athlete).

The sport psychologist who consults with the Olympic athlete must be well aware of drug use, its harmful effects, and the serious consequences to a competitor. The psychologist must consult with team trainers, coaches, and doctors and educate them about drug policy and the problems associated with using IOC-banned substances. In some cases there might be a practical and ethical conflict between the use of a banned substance and one that is prescribed for an athlete who is sick or injured.

KNOWLEDGE AND ACCEPTANCE OF THE RULES

Athletes in international competition must be aware of the drug testing procedure, how it works, and what is expected of them. Under new regulations, athletes will be required to give a urine specimen at random any time during any year, including major competitions such as the Pan-American or Olympic Games. The sport psychologist must keep athletes informed of drug policy, testing procedures, and protocol to follow in case an athlete must take a prescribed medication. For example, before the Seoul 1988 games, a swimmer was disqualified during the trials in Austin, Texas, for traces of a steroid found in her birth control medication, Ortho-Novum. After several appeals to the Olympic committee, she was not permitted to join the U.S. team and compete in Seoul.

Some athletes arrive at a competition and learn that random drug testing is in effect for that day and suddenly they develop a cramp, a flu, or have breathing problems. These psychosomatic complaints are usually in reaction to the fact that in due course their urine will test positive for a banned substance. One of our Olympians told us:

> "So this guy took steroids as an equalizer. It puts everybody on the same ground. Well, we are all looking for improvements and that's the way it is done in East and West Europe. I mean everybody got their dose. Everybody had the right information. Everybody knew how to do it. Everybody had a doctor, you know, or a researcher or a coach that knew what was going on. It wasn't any of this stuff where you can buy it in the gym or you buy it on the street or at the high schools. It was part of a very complex, very scientifically researched program that I imagine is something like putting the man on the moon. There were no accidents . . . everything happened for a reason" (Anonymous athlete).

Some of the prevention and intervention strategies that a sports medicine or psychological consultant might use when confronting a potential substance abuse problem are the following:

• First and foremost, inform the athlete that there is no empirical evidence in the scientific literature that shows steroids to be a performance enhancer.

- If an athlete is using a steroid to heal an injury (which is often the case), educate the athlete about its harmful effects and ask that a physician be present to discuss long-term adverse effects.
- Discuss with an athlete and team members the ethical problems of using performance enhancers. Aside from the legal consequences, is it fair and truly competitive?
- Be sure that, if an athlete is using a drug, the sport psychologist gets informed consent to discuss with a medical doctor, team trainer, and family members the potential problems involved.
- Suggest that an athlete use alternative strategies such as positive imagery and visualization for healing an injury to reduce the need for drugs.
- Discuss with all athletes their role of providing positive peer pressure to prevent substance abuse. If an athlete is already experimenting with or using steroids, encourage peers and friends to offer support and confront the athlete about physical and emotional changes that might be taking place.
- Know the rules and regulations of the governing body, and be familiar with the new procedures of the Olympic Committee. When in doubt use the USOC drug hotline.

The above-mentioned recommendations are essential when counseling an Olympian who might already be experimenting with banned substances. A few hours after the International Olympic Committee met to disqualify Ben Johnson, the National Broadcasting Company carried a live interview with Frank Shorter and Dwight Stones who were in Seoul as official commentators for the network. In discussing the rumor that Ben Johnson's water bottle had been sabotaged, Mr. Stones noted that during Olympic competition, no matter how thirsty one gets, one never borrows water from another competitor. Mr. Shorter, a renowned marathoner and former gold medalist in the event, is also a lawyer, and provided an interesting legal insight. Shorter noted that there is not a due process procedure in international Olympic competition. When an athlete enters Olympic competition, the athlete agrees to and signs a waiver to abide by international rules and regulations. Athletes must then play by those international rules. They are not permitted to go into court and offer a defense based on American jurisprudence. Athletes must know what the boundaries and parameters of Olympic competition are. Professional sports consultants, coaches, and psychologists may assist them with this guidance and understanding (Shorter, 1988).

> "I think that the random drug testing that came into operation this year has cut substance abuse nearly 80 percent. And I think the cross-check verification with other nations will cut abuse even more . . . because the distances have all come down in the throwing events and new world records aren't quite as frequent this year" (Anonymous athlete).

References

Almond, E., Cart, J., & Harvey, R. (1984, January 29). Olympians finding the drug test a snap. *Los Angeles Times*, p. 76.

Altman, L. K. (1988, September 28). Athletes' steroid use causing deep concern. *New York Times*, p. 22.

American College of Sports Medicine. (1984). Position stand on the use of anabolic-androgenic steroids in sports.

Anderson, W. A., & McKeag, D. B. (1985). *The substance use and abuse habits of college athletes* (Drug Education Committee monograph). East Lansing: Michigan State University College of Human Medicine. NCAA Athletic Association Council Executive Committee.

Beckett, A. H., & Cowan, D. A. (1979). Misuse of drugs in sport. *British Journal of Sports Medicine, 12,* 185–94.

Bloch, S., & Ungerleider, S. (1987). Targeting high risk groups on campus for alcohol and drugs: An examination and assessment. *International Journal of the Addictions, 23,* 3.

Brown, H. C. (1989). *Anabolic steroids and testosterone abuse in athletes.* Paper presented at TAC conference for United States Olympic Committee.

Burkett, L. N., & Falduto, M. T. (1984). Steroid use by athletes in a metropolitan area. *Physician and Sports Medicine, 12,* (8), 69–74.

Burt, J. J. (1987). Drugs and the modern athlete: The legacy of Lenny Bias and Don Rogers. *Journal of Physical Education Recreation and Dance, May/June,* 74–79.

Caudill, B., Kantor, G., & Ungerleider, S. (1990). Project Impact: A national study of high school substance abuse intervention training. *Journal of Alcohol and Drug Education, 35,* 2.

Chappell, J. N. (1987). Drug use and abuse in athletics. In J. R. May & M. J. Asken (Eds.), *Sport psychology: The psychological health of the athlete.* New York: PMA Publishing.

Clarke, K. S. (1984). Sports medicine and drug control programs of the U.S. Olympic Committee. *Journal of Allergy and Immunology, 73,* 740–44.

Coward, V. (1987). Classifying steroids as controlled substances suggested to decrease athletes' supply, but enforcement could be a major problem. *Journal of the American Medical Association, 257,* 3029.

Cramer, R. B. (1985, February). Olympic cheating: The inside story of illicit doping and the U.S. cycling team. *Rolling Stone,* pp. 25–30.

Duda, M. (1984). Drug testing challenges college and pro athletes. *The Physician and Sportsmedicine, 12,* (11), 109–18.

Goldman, B. (1984). *Death in the locker room.* South Bend, IN.: Icarus Press.

Goldman, R. (1985). Liver carcinoma in an athlete taking anabolic steroids. *Journal American Osteopathic Association, 85,* (2), 56.

Janofsky, M. (1988, October). U.S. committee adopts drug plan. *New York Times,* 22.

Janofsky, M. (1989). Results plus; track and field rivals meet. *New York Times.*

Janofsky, M., & Alfano, P. (1988, November). Victory at any cost: Drug pressure growing: A five-part series. *New York Times,* p. 21.

Johnson, W. O., & Moore, K. (1988, September 24). The loser; Special report. *Sports Illustrated,* pp. 26–34.

Kleiner, S. M., Calabrese, L. H., Fielder, K. M., Naito, H. K., & Skibinski, C. I. (1989). Dietary influences on cardiovascular disease risk in anabolic steroid-using and nonusing bodybuilders. *Journal of the American College of Nutrition, 8,* (2), 109–19.

Lamb, D. R. (1984). Anabolic steroids in athletics: How well do they work and how dangerous are they? *American Journal of Sports Medicine, 12,* 31.

Mandell, A. J. (1979). The Sunday syndrome: A unique pattern of amphetamine abuse indigenous to professional football. In D. Smith, et al. (Eds.), *Amphetamine use, misuse and abuse* (pp. 218–27). Boston: G. K. Hall & Co.

Neff, C. (1989, September). Scorecard: Drugs and track. *Sports Illustrated,* p. 76.

Penn, S. (1988, October 4). As ever more people try anabolic steroids, traffickers take over. *Wall Street Journal,* p. 16.

Pentz, M. (1985). Social competence and self-efficacy as determinants of substance use in adolescence. In S. Schiffman & T. Wills (Eds.), *Coping and substance use.* New York: Academic Press.

Percy, E. C. (1980). Chemical warfare: Drugs in sports. *Western Journal of Medicine, 133,* 478–84.

Physicians' Desk Reference. (1990). Oradell, NJ: Medical Economics.

Pope, H. G., Jr., & Katz, D. L. (1988). Affective and psychotic symptoms associated with anabolic steroid use. *American Journal of Psychiatry, 145,* 487–90.

Ryan, A. J. (1984). Causes and remedies for drug misuse and abuse by athletes. *Journal of the American Medical Association, 252,* 517–19.

Shorter, F. (1988). Conversations with Frank Shorter at Olympic Games in Seoul, personal communications with SU.

Tennant, F., Black, D. L., & Voy, R. O. (1988). Anabolic steroid dependence with opiod-type features. *New England Journal of Medicine, 319*, (9), 578.

Tricker, R., & Cook, L. (1990). *Athletes at risk: Drugs and sport.* Dubuque, IA: Wm. C. Brown.

Ungerleider, S. (1986). *Drugs in sport,* Research Monograph prepared for the Olympic Committee, Division of Sports Medicine, ERIC NO. RIEFEB88.

Ungerleider, S., & Bloch, S. (1987). Chapter leadership profiles among citizen activists in the drunk driving movement. *Journal of Alcohol and Drug Education, 33,* 1.

Ungerleider, S., & Bloch, S. (1988). Perceived effectiveness of drinking driving countermeasures: An evaluation of MADD. *Journal of Studies on Alcohol, 49,* (2).

Ungerleider, S. & Caudill, B. (in press). Impact: An early intervention demonstration project. In J. Swisher (Ed.), *Experience with high risk youth.* Washington, D.C.: Office of Substance Abuse Prevention, Public Health Service.

U.S. Department of Justice. Drug Enforcement Agency (1988). *Drugs of abuse,* Washington, D.C.: Government Printing Office.

Vecsey, G. (1984). [Interview with NCAA] *New York Times.*

Voy, R. O. (1986). Illicit drugs and the athlete. *American Pharmacology, 2,* (11), 39–45.

Voy, R. O. (1990). *Drugs, sport and politics.* Champaign, IL: Leisure Press.

Zemper, E. (1991). Drug testing: *Issues and options.* Drug testing in athletes. Eds. Robert H. Coombs and Louis J. West. Oxford University Press, NY. 113–39.

Index

frequency of, *51*
lucid, *44–45*
of participation, *49–50*
psychoanalytic approaches,
    39–41
psychophysiological
    approaches, *43–44*
of success, *52–53*
theories of, *38*
Drugs and education, *129*
Drugs and sport, *118, 120–21*
Drugs and student athletes, *123*
Drugs, categories of
    anabolic steroids, *128–29*
    beta blockers, *126*
    blood doping, *127–28*
    depressants, *125*
    diuretics, *127*
    human growth hormone, *127*
    narcotic and non-narcotic
        analgesics, *126*
    stimulants, *124*

E
Everett, Danny, *22, 31, 50,
    85–86, 113*

F
Fear of failure, *101–2*
Feltz and Landers, *17, 18*
Female athletes, *8, 29, 51, 54,
    69, 84, 106, 108–110*
Field athletes, *9, 32*
Fosbury, Dick, *xiii–xiv*
Freud, Sigmund, *39–40*

G
Groos, Margaret, *29, 32–33, 37,
    54–55, 90*

H
Health and Daily Living Form,
    108
HIPS, *82*
HIV infection, *128*
Huber, Vicki, *27, 49, 69, 71–72,
    106*
Human subjects, *7*

I
Iceberg Profile, *63, 68*
Imagery
    ability and control, *19*
    characteristics of, *26*
    external, *18*
    internal, *18*
    kinesthetic, *18*
    visual, *18*
Imagery and visualization, *14*
IMPACT, *133*
Injury and team selection, *90–91*
International Olympic
    Committee, *130*

J
Jansen, Dan, *5*
Johnson, Ben, *118–19, 121,
    128–29, 135*
Jordan, Michael, *74*
Jung, Carl, *40–41*

K

Kinder, Gary, *99*
Konzag, Gerd, *4*

L

Lawrence, Don and Debbi, *91, 104*
LES-A, *81*

M

Male athletes, *8, 69, 84, 106*
Marathon athletes, *9*
Masters track and field athletes, *20–21, 47, 50, 52, 63, 104–5, 107–8*
Mental practice
　clarity of, *27*
　frequency of, *24*
　predictors of, *21*
　timing of, *25*
Mood and injury, *89–90*
Mood research on
　crew and rowing, *65*
　speed skaters, *66*
　swimmers, *66*
　track and field athletes, *65*
　wrestlers, *64*
Moods of athletes, *61*
Moore, Kenny, *119, 129*
Moos, Rudolf, *103*
Murphy, Shane, *4*

N

New York Times, *5*
Non-olympians, *29–30, 70–71, 94*

O

Ogilvie, Bruce, *4*
Olympians, *29–30, 70–71, 94*
Overtraining and staleness, *67–68, 72, 75*

P

Pagel, Ramona, *70–71, 75*
Perceptions of stress, *105–6*
Performance enhancement, *4, 118–19, 123, 127*
Plumer, PattiSue, *51, 73–74, 87–89, 93–94, 112–13*
Prevention, *73, 132–33*
Price, Connie, *108*
Professional vs. amateur athletics, *132*
Profile of mood states, *63–68*
Psyching up theory, *17*
Psychoneuromuscular theory, *17*

R

Raiport, Grigori, *5*
Random testing, *130–31*
　urinalysis, *131*
REM sleep, *43*
Rogers, George, *118*
Russian success method, *5*

S

Sample characteristics, *8–10*
Sample sizes, *7–8*
SARRS, *80–83*
Self-monitoring, *26*
Shorter, Frank, *128, 135–36*
Singer, Ken, *23*
Slaney, Mary Decker, *14*

Social integration, *104*
Social resources, *104*
Social support, *104*
Sports Illustrated, *123–24, 129*
Sports medicine, *22–23*
Sports psychologist, *4, 133*
SRRS, *80–83*
Staleness and burnout, *72, 74*
Stanozolol, *119*
Stones, Dwight, *24, 135*
Stress and injury, *88–89*
Stress and risk factors, *84, 100*
Stressful life events, *80*
Survey research, *7*
Symbolic learning theory, *17*

T
Testing procedures for drug use, 130–31
Track athletes, *9*
Troncoso, Carmen, *61, 93*

V
Vealey, Robin, *15*
Vecsey, George, *124*
VMBR, *15–16*
Voy, Robert, *119*

W
Wilkins, Mac, *20, 27, 92*